BY JOHN YAU

POETRY AND PROSE

Crossing Canal Street (1976)
The Reading of an Ever-Changing Tale (1977)
Sometimes (1979)
The Sleepless Night of Eugene Delacroix (1980)
Broken Off by the Music (1981)
Corpse and Mirror (1983)
Radiant Silhouette: New & Selected Work 1974–1988 (1989)
Big City Primer (1991) (Photographs by Bill Barrette)
Edificio Sayonara (1992)
Lowell Connector (1993) (with Clark Coolidge, Michael Gizzi,
   Bill Barrette, and Celia Coolidge)
Berlin Diptychon (1995) (Photographs by Bill Barrette)
Hawaiian Cowboys (1995)
Forbidden Entries (1996)

MONOGRAPHS

Forrest Bess (1988)
Brice Marden: A Vision of the Unsayable (1988)
A. R. Penck (1993)
In the Realm of Appearances: The Art of Andy Warhol (1993)
Ed Moses: Paintings and Drawings 1951–1996 (1996)
The United States of Jasper Johns (1996)

EDITOR

The Collected Poems of Fairfield Porter (1985)
   (with David Kermani)

JOHN YAU

FORBIDDEN ENTRIES

BLACK SPARROW PRESS • SANTA ROSA • 1996

FORBIDDEN ENTRIES. Copyright © 1996 by John Yau.

ACKNOWLEDGMENTS

Grateful acknowledgment is made to the editors and publishers who first gave these poems a home. MAGAZINES: *American Letters and Commentary, American Poetry Review, Asian American Pacific Journal, Bug House, Columbia Review, Cutbank, Five Fingers Review, First Intensity, Frame Work, Gulf Coast, Hambone, lacanian ink, Lingo, Long News: In the Short Century, New American Writing, Occident, Open City, Plum Review, Postmodern Culture, Prose Poem: An International Journal, Prosodia, Shantih, Talisman, Tea Leaves.* LIMITED EDITIONS: *Picadilly or Paradise* (Ferriss Editions); *Dream Hospital* (Jacob Samuels); *Mon Alias, Mona Lisa* (Generations Colectif), *Genghis Chan: Private Eye* (The Art Institute of Chicago). ANTHOLOGIES AND CATALOGS: *A Curious Architecture: A Selection of Contemporary Prose Poems*, eds. Rupert Loydell and David Miller (Stride, 1996), *Transforming Vision: Writers on Art*, ed. Edward Hirsch (The Art Institute of Chicago and Bullfinch, 1994), *Ronald Bladen: Drawings and Sculptural Models*, Douglas Dreishspoon (Weatherspoon Art Gallery, 1995), *Premonitions; A Kaya Anthology of North American Asian Poetry*, ed. Walter Lew (Kaya Press, 1996), *On A Bed of Rice: An Asian American Erotic Feast*, ed. Geraldine Kudaka (Anchor Books, 1995).

LIBRARY OF CONGRESS CATALOGING-IN-PUBLICATION DATA

Yau, John, 1950–
   Forbidden entries / John Yau
     p.   cm.
   ISBN 1-57423-016-6 (pbk.: alk. paper) — ISBN 1-57423-017-4 (cloth trade: alk. paper) — ISBN 1-57423-018-2 (cloth signed: alk. paper)
   I. Title.
PS3566.A9F67   1996
811'.54—dc20   96-34689
                                    CIP

Table of Contents

I.

II.

III. HOLLYWOOD ASIANS

IV.

V.

I

Variations on a Sentence
by Laura (Riding) Jackson

There is something to be told about us for the telling of which we all wait. Something to be told. There is something about the telling of which we all wait to be told. Something telling. About something which we all wait for the telling to be told. Something about the wait. The telling of something is there to be told. Something about us for the telling. We all wait for the something to be told. The telling is there for us. Something telling is to be told about us. The telling wait. The wait telling us about the told. The wait is something for all the telling. Something to be told about us which is for the telling. Something for us. Something for the wait. Something told for the telling. All we told is something about the us which is there. We wait to be told about the us which is telling something. All is there for the telling of which is there to be told. All is something to be told. All telling is something told about us for which we wait. All of something which we wait for. All telling told. All of us telling wait to be told something. There is the telling to be told. The something told, the something us, the something telling. Something telling is there. There telling us to be told something for which we wait. There is for the telling something of which we wait to be told. Something about us for the wait. Something about the telling to be told. To be something is to wait to be told. Is there something about us for which we wait? About telling us we all wait for something. The telling and the told, the we and us which wait. Us telling which wait is there to be told. Which telling is to be told. Told there is something about us. Told there is the wait. Told of the wait which is something about us. We all told about something. Which something about us for the telling?

The us for which we wait? Which there is something we all wait for? Something of which we tell. There is wait to be told, there is the telling about us. The told something, the telling there. For the wait, the telling us. For the told is for the telling. Wait for the telling to be told. Something for which we wait, the telling to be telling.

The Sculptor Whispers in the Sleeping Poet's Ear
(for Ronnie Bladen 1918–1988)

Leonardo knew the wings of birds would one day be worn by men, that they were destined to lift their shadows above the clouds. But those who thought flight had to do with motion were wrong. It comes from sitting still and watching yourself climb the tilting and turning ladder of stars, your shifting spine, and trembling leaf veins, from following the molecular drift. Who knows where we go when we are gone? All those messages that have been written down, who knows how to read them? Where they came from or who they were meant for? Only a fool thinks that he stands straight.

Now, if you're starting to think this is a message, you're wrong. I'm not a messenger, but a receiver, a crystal radio. I lift into the light the things that someone left behind, someone who wanted to point to where he had been and how he got there. With the kind of precision which does not derive its forms from a book, but from dancing alone, knowing the music will melt only once. It is not a where you can find on a map. It is not the memory of a body of such exquisite pro-portion that I tried to praise its gravity or defiance. I am not that he, hammer and chisel clutched in calloused hands, nor am I even the one speaking softly to you now. The speaker in your dream. This is what you must one day understand. What I did was neither mine nor yours. The world is not that small.

I didn't go from here to there, marking the path of my passage into history. Neither did my sculptures. That way is for liars and thieves, for the ones who cannot leave the room and become the tears of tomorrow's stars documenting their own evaporation.

I am not an engineer, a designer of bridges, though I could have built one if I wanted to. Yes, I could have raised its glistening steel arch over a surging river, like the back of a cat, but I didn't want the language of animals infiltrating my work. Nor did I try to shift the wind's shadows to the precincts of purity and mathematics. After all, I am an earthworm and a clump of dirt, a wet tablecloth and a scuffed floor. Why would I leave this evidence behind, as if my hands left no mark when I pressed them against a mirror?

Just as I now am what is passing through this moonless night, its cold circular hallway. My objects rise from the moment they occupy, they are neither monuments nor houses. The moment is a river, that is what the old Greek told me in a dream. I didn't need to have the same dream twice.

Self-Portrait with Bruno Taut

An infernal fluttering? I don't know
A man can be a liar through and through

He can even go beyond a liar's far flung
diner of ideas and experience

For, like white lice and black wasps,
he makes a durable substance

that forms itself into the turrets
of an invisible fortress

rising above the ledges and leaps of fear
You see, it has always been difficult

to criticize the coprolites of reptiles
or to pass one's excrement

neatly onto the proper scales
I derived my concert hall

from ears of summer corn
stacked like clouds

in the northern sky
It was one way of encouraging the chimney age

to go up in smoke
while still urging

the bacillus of lust to surpass
all nine levels of manual dexterity

Can we discuss I in you and you in me
Have we not started drifting

in the swelling curls of brackish thoughts
which is more than our usual waywardness

As musical notes are crimson bubbles
ripening on branches of exhalation

one must try to develop
an autonomous structural existence

become a sleeve of music
unraveling the wind

In the normal pages of daylight's unfolding
blue provides the deepest possible accompaniment

Let us descend once more
to the roots of this violin tree

and weigh and measure
what our mortal pincers yield

Maggots are dromedaries from Andromeda
I have reached the buoyant part of the forest

where houses grow on trees
like untainted polysyllables

spilling out of air's terraced cortex
Spherical greetings of a luminous city

reflected in rinsed water
New shoes placed by the side of the road

I arrive like a film
with winged feet

blood marking the path
The historian's telescope

gropes in dust
forsaken by mummified cubes

Between one-sidedness and universality
lies a question: I don't understand

your point of view
What about a coin

or a medallion's fourth side
its ticking heart

Shouldn't stars start
igniting the sky

now that the world is rigid
earthen, yesterday

Aren't grasps of breath
invading our throats

Conversation at Midnight

Did I tell you about the couple who slipped into the well?
They got tired of proofreading the town daily,
its expanding parcels of bungalow ooze and unregistered
    adults
that they had to freeze into orderly stems and vintage sequins.
The window was always glued down. You knew that.
I am sorry about the lump I left in your throat.
It was the latest joke someone sent me from another state.
Why did you say I was a camel when you meant something
    else?
There is supposed to be a fiber that will either
make it grow or make them flow. What do you mean
you have already been stapled to a post?
I would gladly accept your garnished buckets
if you had some twitching sauce as well.
It was the pluck of the claw if you ask me, which you weren't.
I will kiss your glue, but I will not miss your shoe.
One slipped through a slot, the other formed a neighborhood
    cult.
There is a rumor they preferred it gloved in steel.
Perhaps you would like to shift your flippers a bit,
make yourself more pungent than a fist clinging
to the grains of its last silver collar.
How would I know what kind of rust coats the inside of my
    dome?
You were always the expert on the proper insect retrieval
    systems,
the necessary buzz tones to pendulum through the hair.
It depends on where you place the nylon and what you plan
    to do

with the extra row of teeth you keep beneath the other pillow.
Let us dust our nubs beneath the guardhouse beams, but this
    time
you be the crust and I will play the tropical raincoat.
You are not. I have lots of botched sobs in my cart too.
There is no need to pull the wings off what is certain.
It depends on when the one that marks the day begins to
    descend.
Don't talk to me like I am some style of perishable food
and you are the only minimum page burner around here.
I have all rinds of dirt. You want to tree some up or what.
Sonar finally brought them through the last truculent gates.
Why do they bang like that if they are not yours to keep.
If you want to lease me, go ahead and cry. You little parking
    lot.

Hospital Parking Lot Rendezvous

Eviscerated bugs were once weathervanes for astronomers,
and flowers grew wherever their burnished boots landed.
So how did we get caught in this swamp of drowning birds?
The only voice I heard was the one floating in my coat.
Was it because the sun's postcard
was leaning against the horizon?
and the pulmonary machines had to be started over.
Why dedicate your rudeness to others?
Sure, we could have used one of the hours
we tunneled in a parallel life,
on a mopped beach facing a bankrupt volcano,
its tumbling huts and rusty falls.
But why cross the road when you're a chicken?
The wind has started nestling into
the fat swirls of the third and fourth sky,
insect trammeled corridors,
and abandoned parade booths.
I collect wings. What did you bring home
besides notebooks full of spit and boils?
I was always careful with the headlights
mounted on your advertisements,
seaweed swollen benches and metal whiskers
pouring through society's sieve.
Every morning, lines of yapping flags spotted the air.
Yes, I believe in charcoal dust and secret hand signals,
but I don't know any characters or assassins,
only the empty raisin boxes they have left behind.
Would you like me to read your calm?
You were the dog and I was the drooping fence
you ran beside, your milky tongue lapping

the last shreds of breeze walled above
morning's stillness, like a movie
that has lost all its shadows.
You think you can fake it on your own?
Be the dirty leather windmill,
the dripping yellow bicycle.
I was an adopted fan who yearned to grunt.
I was a bridge over which drunken hornets gathered.
I was a speckled cloud lolling in moustache filth.
These things I told myself
as if I was the one who was listening,
my cauliflower flap pressed to the door of medals.
We all cry in our fear sometimes.
It's the puddle we grew up in.
If only you had told me about what you wore
beneath your prison tunic, its wings of recovered grime.
If only I had listened to the spells
bending the day. I was a picture
before I was a boulder
before I balanced on a ledge,
a long red rung without a ladder.

Hoboken Palace Gardens

We sat beneath a webbed and vaulted sky,
listening to the mechanical mockingbirds

live up to their name.
A green and white cab came and waited

until the last bullet was swept up
and put in a transparent envelope.

The old driver puffed on a red cigar
which he said he found in the library.

Two nurses wrapped me in a pink blanket.
The fat one handed my sister a plastic bone.

After the bricks unraveled and the tornado
collapsed on the outskirts of town,

like an old man whose anger
has finally stabbed him,

the story gets progressively colder.
A man stood up and peed in his coffee cup.

Wanda got a job with the rodeo as an assistant cook,
and Purple Bill finally learned

why his neighbors called him "Esmerelda Desdemona"
when he started his fancy jalopy.

I could have told you another white lie.
I could have heaped it on the mountain

gathering before you. Perhaps it would have
even been the truth, the whole truth,

but I wouldn't have known it, not then and not now.
When the air gets thick and stuffy like this

my brain turns into a dog dish I circle,
my tongue hanging out like a wet flannel sleeve.

I wore your underwear to work the other day
but it didn't make me feel as sexy as I thought it would.

Why have you stopped tapping your foot?
I was just beginning to get in the mood

to swing down from my branch and sing.
That sweet smell is the soup starting to rot.

I am, as always, your disobedient servant.

Two Aztecs from New Jersey

I don't know what else to attribute it to,
but I think we each have two different sets of personalities.
Yesterday, you submitted an appended roster of vital statistics
to the uptown breeding contest, and tomorrow one of us
will enter our names in the registry
for future celebration and imminent disposal.
We like the hoopla, but not the late night apologies
draped in syndicated provender.
Perhaps the foil could be tinted a different color
and not reek of caloric melancholy and asteroid indifference.
Is this the inaugural gown you promised me?
or another informative sculpture
I am supposed to install beside our basalt hearth?
its tower of penetrated electric logs.
What is this surface over which giants fight and fall?
I like the one you burned better than the one you kissed.
Polish off a tumbler of sour cherry wine without the cherries
and you'll be dancing on the graves of your grandchildren
before you know it. Isn't that how our lullaby scurried out
over the airwaves, undulated down simulated turnpikes,
swaying above grease spots and skid marks?
The bandaged badinage we spiked to whip up the morning
    froth.
Whatever happened to Lily the Selfish Elf, Old Bark,
and Stumpy Jane, a blond whoosh
who thought paintbrushes were chopsticks with beards?
Remember the plastic face we hired to rub our bellies,
back when bellies were trophies you could swing by the hair.
Remember the radical tissues we chomped on with gusto,
the gulps of vinegar and vulgarity we used

to conclude our sessions. And don't forget the brass spittoon
where our neighbor planted his uncle's velvet lunge.
Someone famous bought it at an auction,
says he uses it as an ice bucket for Sunday brunch.
Whatever happened to the autobiographical waste
we were stockpiling in the driveway?
Surely one of our effusive, chartered clones must know
what hideous snowstorm each of us will soon become.
A hot, bumpy bus ride to the renovated part of town.
A disheveled louse swinging in the next seat,
salaried sweat oodling through his pockmarked moonface.
A convention hall that looks like a sun hat for a snake.
Carpets of glittering asphalt to greet you
when you step from your rented carriage.
Didn't you once say that we were much happier
when we were as shallow as the graves of murdered children?
that back then there were no pestiferous swarms gumming up
        our sack race
from the satellite channels of Old Mister Daylight.

The Executioner Meets Mister Ball and Chain

Become the next armload of fuzzy headlocks and iron bunny
    hugs?
Learn to sigh and divide beneath the axe of inflected inquiry?
I'm not as gullible as your little louse clock,
its circle of smiling rats in red bandanas.
I'm not even as susceptible as the subcutaneous lichen
    oozing beneath your newspaper smile,
you tumescent vat of grimy scales warmed over pickled hyena
    spit.
You might as well be a bag of chocolate swirls
stuck to a dirty ceiling in a desert motel.
Soon the auditor will come and take your pulse.
Why cuddle a tarred steer or sweet talk other steamy residue
when there are droves of mangy clumps swatting televisions
in all the bus stations in Indiana?
I like Indiana. I used to go there
and hop about on a wooden leg,
looking for signs of gophers and other derailed vermin,
but now that I've earned a degree in holistic projection
you can only chase my mirage,
one of those green flannel shirts
you used to see floating above a lake,
moonlight streaming through the singing bullet holes.
I once thought of you as a little rubber sombrero,
because you protected me from the glare of one-eyed giants,
their lamps screwed into the mouths of scrawny children.
We tangoed beside the rented refrigerator and laughed.
We slurped cotton vines from thin bottles.
We didn't send money to the slim man on TV
who spoke through the nightgown of his reincarnated wife.

But now that I have you curled up in a vulture armchair,
it might be time for you to start sucking rocks.
That's what thirsty dogs do when they find themselves
stuck on a traffic island between two warring clans.
You can't crawl under my velvet doormat and hide once more.
My feet are planted there, like a policeman's belly.
You can't pretend your mind didn't wander off
and never returned, leaving me with a pail of bronze bulk.
My noggin has been registering the aftershocks of winter's
    chill
while you and I chop through the clumps of dirty air
collecting in the thuds of our public discussions.
Rub this globe and feel the tapeworm music vibrating in the
    bumps.

Castor and Pollux

1.

I don't know why I became a fiend and you didn't.
Like you, I was born in an old warehouse by the docks,
but, unlike you, I have no memory of the mold clinging to
    my bib
as I crammed my mouth full of oyster porridge
and dribbled kefir down my chin. Perhaps
the road I took did start with my parents' penchant for wine
with every meal, including their breakfast of
fresh plums, warm pumpkin rolls, and pickled herring.
But now they are no more than a profile of blue clouds
sinking below the tablecloth's horizon
or a silk sleeve caught in a burning door.
What kind of remarks return you to your childhood?
the slate wall where you first let your hands
open someone else's secret desk. And what will you
or can you bequeath to that or any other space,
which you can no longer fill?

2.

One of them wore a moustache, the other a nightgown made
    of ties.
Their biographer claims lava flowed from every flower
they planted in their bedroom of capricious delights.
In the museum is the tattered camisole she wore
the day the telegram was delivered by a man wearing tin
    wings.
Can I read your palm, the one with the valentine tattoo?

Of course, it's a fossil. That's why you are keeping it safe
within the curtains you were blessed by the wind to wear.
Someone somewhere is always puzzled by what is said.
A row of pigs is lined up before a piano.
One of them must always be the donkey when the other
is on the balcony, waiting for the film to start.
What is this? a voice on the golf course cries out,
the latest pebble added to the mound of sob glory?
Or just another bald-hearted attempt to pry open my sighs?

3.

Hey Brittle Cruiser, if you want to make mustard with me,
you have to slay the monkey judge and steal his robes.
Maybe unravel the dresses and hats of his sisters as well.
It is not my hair or skin I want to bleach, but my mind.
They liked to fill a room with crumpled paper before entering
     it.
Something about hearing their shadows speak to them
before they fall, something about wanting to feel the ground
yield its words to them when they walk, roll, or crawl,
something about lightning music and long whips of honeyed
     smoke.
Have you ever seen yourself on television? That's one way
we might start rehearsing the concerts you say you've written.
Will you retrieve me from the pawnshop when I am cold and
     stale?
Will you polish me the way you used to, with borrowed
     hands?
Even if part of you was stuck inside a bottle,
like a genie with no strings attached to my ankles,
I don't know if I would do exactly what you want.
What journal do you have in the mind?
The one between your teeth or the one you cannot breathe.

The Newly Renovated Opera House
on Gilligan's Island

Between the hastily sketched chalk curtains a backdrop of yellow cliffs and avalanche mist rising toward a quarter moon. The old, bearded shepherd, who is famous for his reenactments of the early torments of bruised tots, stands up and points to the baloney stains on his shirt, each word forming like a soap bubble on the craters of his huge, cracked, green lips. A bamboo sewing machine monitors the smell of rotten food trapped beneath the snow. Sound of a train compartment window being opened, accompanied by a foreign, possibly threatening language, gutturals mixed with sand and glass. Guided by pulleys, four ebony sticks roll two purple cabbages painted like salesmen's bruised brains down the aisle of the third class coach. A murderous scream is heard in the balcony causing the audience to turn away from the stage, which a moment later is illuminated by red searchlights. A piece of slightly charred synthetic material, mostly white, floats to the floor. A woman, who is a weathered wooden tower, gazes at the horizon, while the sounds of lovesick whales become increasingly louder. At first she appears diffident, but it is soon quite obvious that she has spent the past few hours sobbing into a large damp hanky, which she occasionally wrings out with machine-like efficiency. A man limps onto the stage and squints up at the creaking tower. He begins a lengthy monolog of scabrous insults mixed with detailed comments about animal infidelity and the recent invasion of earth by creatures who resemble child movie stars. When he finishes, he falls to his knees and fishes two jade green marbles from his vest pocket. For the first time the woman notices him and says: You little punctured zygote. How dare you fondle your sprockets in my presence. Heed my warning or you will end your days drooling over yourself and your tarnished brood of loved ones. You will live long enough to see your grandchildren dwelling among ants, smaller than the ones that come to feed them bits of meat held between shiny black pincers.

Kneeling amidst the cool winds undulating across the stage, the man pays no attention to the woman's lava of accusations, its bubbles of ochre bombast. There are other bursts to consider, particularly since his distinctive, undersized nose has started bleeding, and he finds it impossible to staunch the apparently endless cascade. A pool of brownish liquid forms a small lake, where two women in pink Easter bonnets are drowning. In the illuminated distance, which is separated from the lake by a stone wall built during the reign of a toothless tyrant, three slightly overweight, garrulous policemen are riding silver bicycles. The middle one is carrying a maroon leather bag shaped like a child's head and finds it difficult to maintain his balance. I want to doze while time continues flowing through this planetary circuit I've been saddled with, its butter dish of blinking dreams. My own thoughts are surrounded by embroidered throwaway pillows, and I am little more than a kite string of withered peony petals somersaulting across a kitchen counter. The sky mangled corpse of a doodlebug clings tenaciously to the storm window. The word "stupendous" is carefully printed in turquoise lipstick on the refrigerator's gray enamel door. An empty quinine bottle spins across the counter and stops before reaching the stainless steel sink.

The sand shifts its vertical and horizontal parameters, the music of its grinding spheres broadcasting dented pulses to the scaly creatures hibernating on the irregularly arranged lower shelves. Two tents flatten into a tablecloth of stars once seen floating in the Southern hemisphere. A spotted red-and-orange mongrel begins dancing on its hind legs around the town's last fountain, its disheveled pyramids of poisoned birds. Sheila has been told that a mauve-streaked tornado has carried

33

off all the camels lined up at the Connecticut Taxi Stand, and now fears that she will never be able to find Aunt Jane, who vanished while walking from the hotel to the curio shop in search of old engravings of blind Japanese men to put above her bed. A loudspeaker begins broadcasting a slightly hoarse, porcelain layered voice, which tells the crowd gathered by their windows that there is an iron bridge in the old city that will lead them to various forms of modern transportation, and that all the drivers and engineers will guarantee their passengers the lifelong supply of rejuvenation pills they will need after completing their reentry forms. As a final gesture of both disdain and gratitude, Sheila turns around and begins pulling up her black silk dress and adjusting her lime-green nylon stockings, while licking her lips with an abnormally large purple tongue, which is the most visible result of her having devoured two dozen grape lollipops for breakfast. A huge wooden door closes. Mice scurry back into their holes and flies finally settle near drying food stains. The bald man behind the spotted metal desk goes to the filing cabinet and pulls a jar of earthworms out of the bottom drawer. He turns and opens the closet and begins examining a mound of raincoats, each of which is made from a different colored plastic. A large rubber hand descends from the hologram of a rainbow, which is rising out of the file cabinet's top drawer, and begins making corrections. The movements are simultaneously deft and mannered. Flames are engulfing the curtains and spreading towards the backdrop of windows and wooden shutters. The young, well dressed man, who has been sitting in a leather chair on one side of the stage, crashes to the floor, clearly a stiff. Smoke fills the school cafeteria. Children scream and run in every direction, both disturbed and amused by the sight of their teachers being rapidly and painlessly transformed into the tarnished and chipped tourist items their parents inspect at garage sales. A horde of beggars has crawled over to the dead man and is skimming through his pockets. The leader is whistling a familiar tune that no one in the audience can name. A brand new column of crimson sunlight is being lowered through a convoy of threatening clouds. A faint breeze tingles the air, its fleshy remnants.

Fifty for Richard Nonas

What is it makes this place what it is and nowhere else? What were the things in this room before they became what they are? What makes you think they and the room are separate? What other places are there that might have led to this place? What makes memories into something else? What path did you take to get here? What path will you take to leave? What is this here you are in? What is a path? What makes this what it is? What name will you give it? What names will circle the name you have given it? What will those other names bring you to? What will be the name you don't give it? What is the name of the place you keep your secrets in? What makes these names secrets? What happens in the spaces between seeing and walking? What separates you from this place? What kind of separations do you require before you believe you are where you are? What does walking bring to you? What do you bring to walking inside and outside places you have never been? What are you inside of? What is invisible outside this place you are inside of? What is invisible inside this place you are filling with carbon dioxide? What besides air, light, and memories? What is this what you are seeing and walking in? What are you doing now that you are here? What leads you to believe you are here and nowhere else? What other place is there? What will be different when you leave this place? What will be different about what happened before you entered it? What was done to this place so that it becomes what it is? What wasn't done? What do you feel you need to know now that you are here? What gave you this thought? What will you do with this thought now that it is yours? What place is this and where will it go once you leave it? What happens after you have seen it, as well as walked in it? What joins you to this place so that you will never leave it?

What makes you think you have never been here? What makes you believe you have ever been here? What places do names fill? What place or places does this place fill? What do you do with names that never reach their destination? What do you do with destinations that have no names? What will you do when you leave this place? What will you do before you arrive? What does it mean to arrive? What have you done that you haven't done before? What will you do now that you know that?

One More Excuse

There were neither pillars to pry apart
nor pillows to push together

One pretended to have dreams
about a pink brocade pouch

while the other curled around
a pungent blue radiator

Each felt as if someone had been stranded
on a refurbished traffic island

someone who didn't know what else to do
when skipping through

trumpets of wheat, beneath
long scuffed trails and bronzed wisps

someone who believed whistling
was the only necessary pleasure

Did you see the bubbles trapped in the green dish
they keep locked in the cupboard

They claim it's a family heirloom
shipped from the piers of Baltimore and beyond

Why do some people point to their inheritance
as if an honored voice

is constantly being broadcast through
ant encrusted notes of an amber afternoon

Just because I wear authentic moccasins
doesn't mean I should learn how to talk softly

I keep my banners with my scarf
They kept their sugar in a secret cave

behind the three door garage
and pretended to be statues

whenever a mailman or a dog walked by
I heard the taller one used to be

a second soprano in a mountain town
gleaming pockets and porous rock

Something about the rhythms of his
external disposition leads me to believe

he keeps all their shrieks
folded inside a frozen bag

She was an heiress
as well as an artifact

a weathered stump you dig up
from the mythic past

its menu of lost islands
and dependable poisons

Shall we pretend today is another muggy funnel
we must slide down

Or are you more in tune
with the illuminated muddle

you and I and all our ugly twins
have recently entered

I wanted to be a ribbon rather than a violation
I wanted to be a broken comb rather than a knot

I wanted to be stencil rather than a gnawed stub
Such sentiments held me aloft on sharpened prongs

Hay clings to the pimply elf's borrowed knee-socks
The elevator stops before it breaches the ceiling

where a cloud of characters are displayed
like pyramids of raincoats and sprayed fruit

Each dewy eye and pink ear is a filter
through which leering gods have started to pour

a few drops of their semi-precious nectar
A crowd of drunken nurses are gathered below

shifting like cones of confetti
behind a thin man with polished slats

Furry rowboat ants
worry robot pants

begin streaming into the motel cafeteria
some with gleaming utensils

clutched in their understated mandibles
Do you want to cut the buzzard

and do the swamp muffin stomp
Did you want to say something else

about what happened to us
when we finally left the ocean

and began wearing bells in the house
Climb this cup with me

but watch out for the broken handle
mud sloshing over dented trim

How was I to flow down the tree again
How was I to grab the river you pushed me in

I was a tinfoil star
pinned to a scuffed ball

an innocuous leak that was never nixed
I am a whittled flapjack

a Hackensack cabby
speeding towards the wrong ocean

I may have learned to cling with the others
but I wanted to see myself as a kind of leisure suit

Who was to know you were admitting white collar slime
through your outer membranes

Buffalo and Marshmallows

It's an old glory
when Greta Gabbo

boasts that any tall
thumb tucking

pimple popper
still in touch

with the bottom of his atavistic roots
shall soon be rented out

to the King of Pencil Toads
and his last iron caravan

Dairy wolves howl at empty spoons
while I sleep in back mall

lily padded trailer park
answer the second

second
I'm stalled in a parallel stupor

squeezed between red hurt of a fall potato
and blue stones of a part-time seed shifter

I'm one of the jilted
eager to bite the crust

I plead with what's left of the steam engine
because I know its soft pajamas

being one of the flies
A free sample sniffing around

the tattered drums of effluvial honey
You get to count creamy blots and carpet burns

transmit grains of junked passion
to the weekend handwarmers

west of Sandusky, Ohio
adopted home of tormented petal pushers

one charm boxers and retired log nuts
the whole glad parking lot of idle fun seekers

You even score the church fire
and pray to the invisible camera

You get down on your full grown knees
and you begin to stay

In better times, I lived on a bingo farm
ate off a checkerboard

Each morning, I baked out the stains
and flicked drivel into the yard

Self-Portrait with Unidentified Painting

An emulsion of signal fires
locked between black crags

Smoke drifting to the seven corners
Warehouses of infested lore

Vast vestibules
Forgotten storage units

Murky jars thick with eyes and ears
Peeling stalls, polished steam engines

An emerald web of wavelengths
suspended in a map's icy interior

A field of shifting vectors
and sudden accelerations

Cerulean motions
cadmium glances

ochre retreats
Collisions with the mush

growing on trees
Cannibalism

as the only form of meaningful exchange
left to pursue

A radar screen one assumes
can penetrate the outermost layers of the skull

its thin templates of borrowed skin
draped over the victor

The foreshortened wind and medicinal peasant
Unlikely additions and late subtractions

That there is a way to breach
the barrier of bone

in which each of us is encased
a gelatinous mass indoctrinated with silt

A stippled house with many rooms
and in each of these rooms

a shelf where mashed bugs
and their host dogs

are inebriated on rust
Bobbing multitude of greasy hats

The tongue you bit off
so you would not betray

the one who slides
between wallpaper and forest

between water's wall
and water's shadow

their pages leaking
through the layers of your borrowed hand

a mirror where one sees
the silver self

leaving rows of tear-filled boots behind the door
Attempts to grip motion

before you are hooked to a machine
A dream inscribed above a Latin door

You have been designated
by one of the renegade gods

to return as a gumshoe's
hairy protuberance

an ermine full of vapid ire
a sock preserved in formaldehyde

a brew of yaupon leaves
Why am I holding a spoon full of flies

Something else is leaving this sack
this derelict temporal witness blight

beach fund incinerator
verb noun photon

What happened to my sagging neck
the dented fender of my first tricycle

the broken watch my father gave me
as a lesson in the meaning of time

Suitcase particles
tungsten appendages

The questions: Do I store them
like medals in the Book of Boats

Are memories a passport
Were these the lessons I had to learn

a shaman growing up among dotted rats
guided by each of my invisible

sister's imaginary dolls
the ones who drip on command

I was part of a destiny foretold in scarves
Downtown uptown all the world

a club waiting to lure me
into its alley

Inflections and rejections
hung on the lip of every welcome word

Bats trembling in dust laden
elevators of a moonless night

I was where
my parents sagged together

two stories full of ashes
two mouths full of ants

I dropped coffee between
pages of my practiced look

I threw quips at the quick
who charged me with their candles

gestures rising in an eagle scarf
a mangled toadstool tuft

I clogged the batteries of those
who commandeered podiums

I am from the strong side of the slacks
I stole the New Ohio nectar

retired Chaldean elders
stuffed in their red plastic pouches

I exploded dental intersections
but rejected impeccable canines

I scorned those who designed flags
but burned behind the parapet of my lies

I galloped down nullified slopes
I changed numbers on uniforms

so everyone forgot
their professional affiliation

I altered and erased
handprints of blue and yellow dust

while dancing in the Book of the Infinite Continuum
I practiced various forms of erotic breathing

common to the fish
lurking above my dream shelf

I drooled my way down
the evolutionary ladder

leaving models of behavioral tics to others
I scoffed as if all this pointing

reached me in the mirror
where my resemblance once stood

crouched in oil
shot through

with flakes of spit and gold

Picadilly or Paradise

When I leap through the flung-open windows of your dance
and reach toward my shadow, its drifting silk and nylon net,
everyone looks at the wind growing a new set of teeth
                    around the moon.
Once, they were among the sweetest of the town's prize
    apples,
evocative names and histories a waiter would point to on the
    menu,
his mouth forging the budding pink and yellow clouds
that would soon swell and open above the visitor's table.
I remember praying for a dazzling array of snow and clay
to descend the stairs to the cellar where I was kept.
But she was afraid to reveal her latest desire:
blue face powder kept in the bronzed shoe of a former lover,
and velvet gloves for every bird.
                    As for him,
the man with silver breath, words were like a toupee—
something he could not share with anyone.
An ink storm swept across this emblazoned map
where pompous couples prided themselves on their choice
of emerging crowd pleasers and corncob furniture.
A train full of inscribed pavement stones rattled through
the tunnels, its polished bronze instruments
swaying gently in the lower layers of the united dark.
Each of us ends up a piece of luggage carried by others.
When I am on my belly, I am glad that I am not a turtle.
carrying my tiled igloo toward the advancing sea.
You flicked off your wings, but I left them in the sand.
Remember, satisfaction isn't necessarily a guarantee.
I am neither Delilah's niece nor her nephew,

because I keep a pair of scissors beneath my mattress.
A hotel would probably provide the best pillows
for our next little excursion, but I don't like numbered doors.
I like my rooms to have a name: Passionate Chitchat,
Nervous Bells of the Fragile Dawn, Delicate Smothering
Amidst Chrome Snooze Lots, Impersonal Convenience
Of A Kind You Might Not Have Known About Until Now.
I want the reception to remind you of a clean river.
No more metal shutters or rusted fences. I am positive
there are other acceptable forms of rehabilitation
that will entice me to remove my customized fingernails
from your smile, the one you have never worn
when you glide above the bolts of our mortgaged axle.
Why do some screams attract more sightseers than others?
Why do you grip your lips? Why do I grab my sagging slab?
Some questions beg the answer, others anoint their fingers.
Either I am waiting for a sign of permanent eruption
or you are dousing candles in the last yawns of our jury.

The Star-Crossed Duet of Miss Burakumin and Mister Hollywood

O she'll be clomping around the fountain when he drums
and she'll be stomping on the phantom when he dances

A short tropical war unfurls its dirty towel
from the balcony of an upgraded television

its broadcast enhancements imported from
the Golden Age of stench smoothing

I was like you once
a moody slinker full of rain

Then I threw my dog badge into the bushes
and began counting backwards

until I learned to climb
the terraces of corporate lava

and paste the ashes to your lips
with my tongue

You were my tall dish of water

O he'll be flying from the shower when she blinks
and he'll be drying every flower when she weeps

I too have pissed away the milk of many past lives
that's why I spend my mornings

pouring cold gravy
on freshly laundered shirts

Did you ever consider
what the world was like

before you became a silver goon
propped between company spears

You must have temporarily scratched
the tumor of your lessons

and forgotten that the rising sun
is an investment banker

and the yellow moon
a delinquent credit card owner

Yes, I was your sour cherry crumb flake
the residue of worry

tickling your chin

O they'll' be stomping little phantoms when you dance
and they'll be clomping around the fountain when you drum

O soon the world will be dancing on the windows of your thumbs

Bar Orient

Club stork
Stalk red

Slit coat
Slice throat

Faceless animals
Pan brain dish

Shiny slug
The voice of clod

narrates latest
kimono sunset

hullabaloo
Yellow crowds

persimmon sky
jukebox ruby

Lotus diggers
raise another

perfumed slat
on pillow dogs

rolling in
dragon blossom

Dew on the duck
Wage wranglers

flick dust
swirl lemon

Shady grove boys
cropped in floating whirl

Corn dreams
stretched through

planetarium silk
grab sayonara coupons

Iron skirts
starch dollar

Forbidden ditty
Cheong sam can-can

Talking alligators
slum elevator abbatoir

Belly horde shakes
pulley torch

Pearl mimosa
roast swig

Hand unshaven stool
two crisp yards

Good fences
hard find

Spoon music
slip junk

Mule snort
elephant grain

Squamous Dicky Rickshaw
leaves tales of yearning flames

collecting on Hollywood stills
Crooked rookie

loots hot grind
Wan Ringo

marries horse
in penthouse of Augie Goon

Mickey Fang, part throb
with a slung noodle

tangoes in a white
tornado of potato mash

Curse swingers
soothe clap

Business carp sip
straw insect twist

Virgin sushi
peel strangers

while Minnie
volcano rave

in hallway halter
lifts her tray up

sloped fountain
Fan slaves

sit on turtles
Honorary coroners

embroider facade
Blue and red

grass shirts
sway path

through organized smoke
tinkle ivy chopsticks

caress steel thumb
drum ukelele riff

Bamboo spaghetti
Madmen flutter by

Pagoda Jeweler's
fluted rug

Nasty Orders Pacify Queen

Antonia greases limp braids
Billy humps mezzanine contraband
Criticism interrupts nozzle deadline
Depression jargon opens evening
Event kickoff parade forecast
Flounder Lord quashes goblet
Gashes Merlin's reflective ham
Horace neutralizes serious incident
Itinerant orators trounce jinx
Juvenile pecadillos urbane kennel
Kiosk quip vapors legible
Livid research wanderer masticates
Meteor shower xenophobes nullify
Neckline tempo yearning ossification
Office undergoes zephyr plague
Punitive vexations anchor quill
Querulous woodwind buccaneer recital
Renounce xeroxing cheery swigs
Salami yams dill tuna
Turtle zebra eagle unicorn
Uhlan admonishes fulminating veil
Vertiginous blue gladiator wall
Windward caravel hinders xebec
Xylophone duress initiates yank
Yurt eskimo joss ziggurat
Zeppelin flames kindle Antonia

So Much Has Already Happened

I am on the shrapnel inlaid verandah
stalking the flower of your inimitable style

when they begin speaking
They say they are angels

but I know they are just chemical transmissions
my brain has unexpectedly downloaded

One is tall and has a nose like a hat
you would wear in a summer rain

The other has a tongue that clicks like a subway
Bad teeth blink through a fog of foul breath

disappearing around a tumbleweed bend
where they push me from a car

A woman in a sparkling black evening gown
stands in a phone booth making a large bet

I tell her she is the answer
to every man's scream

and then tie the dog to an old tire
I've been known to evaporate

before the jacarandas bloom
There are certain pleasures

no one can escape
This is where there is a rope

that lashes me to the bed
and wings that lift me

from sleep's carcass
so I can see the others

swarming in the grooves
I try counting but lose my place

What did you want to add to the milk
Why do you say the clouds are in a coma

when you know about the artificial pond
filled with plastic frogs

I once told you a story about a corridor
full of broken toys

and a machine that dispensed suppositories
to all latecomers

You saw different colored liquids
flowing through tubes

jars of tears kept for special occasions
Knowing these things, perhaps it's time

you stopped pacing back and forth
and come back into the cold

Epic Bone Hinge

Truffle eager Norsemen set out after Ephraim

Briny flinger stubs and shoulder length wands
Juggle figs find figs knife figs hide figs
Strafe sex ranches before brunch
Knit turkey bone shroud
Block bundle slicks veering toward bedecked monks
Wait until zoo flecks come
Sudden waffle surge
Wrecks sewing in more stacked figs

Fig heater dies in house mine

O dank freighter glitch of my warrior brother
His leaf statue drinks in brute zeal
Camper zigzag trance sprays wild swimmers
Stilled toddler laugh bell hatches mutt pals
Trapped mirror might bait
Fig strafer of our fig rich ground

I am a fig hugging splatter with zipper

Immersed figs of the dry Andes
Six dimmed vortices harass us
Orphans fuse hands on the tattered lasso
And under the hymnal rises the egg yolk
Fig leaf begins its fall — blue fig bombs
One soldier retreats willingly from the church gang
And swabbed lovers fake their spirals

Another corpse is dandled between swills of art
Another fig sticks in the vertical

A big green boater is necessary

Another turbine of figs is fully sorted
Beer drinkers exemplify this corpse stand
All has been licked off the fraulein's velvet bat
Her hands and lungs are declared rust free
Beer marker crisis speeds cost past fire hydrants
I figure another demand for five will do
I speak to the feathers
— their gift of feet soaked in immunity —
On the nature of horizon lust
Parallel ascension within the first inkling
Dog tonic to cool the stare
O the figs of paradise hinder us

Truffle eager Norsemen set out after Ephraim

Ban figs — the coal flavored remedies of our neighbors
Enlivens our fists and charm
Gaudy brethren leaf through first narcotic gauges
Shutterbugs militate against round gleams
An act befitting the rest of the seated ribbons
Store the ice tins beside the lieutenant
Forget the bends in the swizzle sticks
Another trolley uncurls its shimmering roar

Truffle eager Norsemen set out after Ephraim
Their fins clattering against the wind

Blue Lizard Lounge

Do you still think about the little foil park
where we first pounced on each other's foibles

One of us clapped at the wrong time for the wrong reason
I think it was near the converted subway station

where the moon stopped and flared
like an apple tree in irreversible mutation

None of the lessons about manners
and other forms of aquatic adaptation rang true

in the trident hours of our idiopathy
It was at the end of the nuclear age

and the beginning of our second false winter
The man who invented pest control for honeymooners

lay on an aluminum shelf in Armadillo, Texas
someone else's name tag dangling above his nose

like a crumpled Christmas angel
There were times when you twiddled

more than your malefic thumbs
I know there are other tragedies to consider

that the cities are fluttering with lost ghouls
who will leave a shiny taste in your blouse

Haven't I stopped chasing leopard skin paw prints
So why do you still clomp across the floor

Is it the stuffy office warren you spin in
refundable bottles collecting at your swollen feet

All around us retractable mandibles are poised
silvery tongs reflecting

the last traces of the painter's chubby green cherubs
Was he the only one who cut the smiles out of our faces

and pasted them to the shirt of a sullen child
Broken teeth and a bloody lip

I never met a human being who didn't suffer
the comedian announced

as everyone leaned over their tables
and waited patiently for his dirty red toupee

to slip or fall

After a Painting by Jasper Johns

It was only difficult being a corpse when he began forgetting the days preceding the change in his status. Didn't I used to look in the mirror each morning? Wasn't I once something else besides a corpse? But what did I see when I looked in the mirror? and what does it look like when no one is front of it? Is it a corpse of some kind, cold and alone in the shifting light? Why do I remember these words: You cannot become someone else's mirror no matter how hard you try? I am not a corpse, he thought, I am its shadow.

A mirror is a wall you stand in front of in the morning, as well as at night before going to sleep. He thinks: If I am not a corpse, but its shadow, what did I do in the hours that fill the air between sunrise and sunset? Did I go to a room where there was no mirror of any kind? Did the others in that place think I was a corpse? Had one of them been my mirror, would I have been able to see myself as I am now? Perhaps I was a corpse before I became a shadow, a ball which never lands in the brown leather glove flapping below, like a mouth with no teeth. I remember the words, I look in the mirror, but I have no memory of what I said next.

Who do you see when you look at a corpse? I remember the mirror was turned to the wall and that the blinds were drawn. I was a cloud floating above and below a corpse striped by slats of rinsed light filtering into the hazy room; and held my name under his tongue. A mirror is a wall we fail to look at, didn't I say that once? We think that unlike a corpse, it must show us something other than itself. I looked in a mirror and did not see anything that I knew, it was my shadow staring back at me.

But a corpse, I said to my reflection, talks to itself in a language that no one else understands; it is either an idea or something that vanishes before it begins.

If a mirror has no ideas, then what does it say to us? It says:
I am a corpse without a body, a body you want to inhabit, as if it is your own. It says: I mirror the world you are leaving behind, but I am not the place in which you will arrive. It says: A corpse is neither a surface nor a place. And a mirror is a thing one thinks of as both surface and a place. Is this the place, I ask, where the corpse never arrives, the place where I have never been? Or is that both these things mirror each other by becoming more themselves?

Whispers Inside the Garage

He wanted to learn a discipline, but he couldn't decide
which one would make him free enough to plead for more.
She said she was really skinny then, a Saturday newspaper.
I heard they had an interest in salt and other yellow crystals,
things they believed were as palpable as puppies on a pillow.
I like the root cellar, especially when it's fetid.
Do you see these boots? They're made for stalking
the dreams you wish you had when you were a child.
Cast a golden lie, she said, and all your household nicknacks
will turn into little gods; shiny figurines
sweating incense and wisdom in the cluttered rooms
of a vast surburban night, its turnstiles of burning leaves.
What kind of clamps did you mean? The ones
whose hooves carry you to the Library of Forbidden Looks?
Or have I been aiming for the wrong station all along?
like an insect in a wind tunnel.
Some prefer effigies to the real sting.
Others like to seal the monkey stench rising from their
    motors.
Who cares if they know how to navigate or not? What about
    us?
We're just stalled erosions waiting for fate's fat man
to release us from our frozen tunics and cement noose.
Let the puddles recite their visitations from the liars above.
Let the violin show you its long black tongue,
the one that flows across the wires wrapped around your neck.
I was a Coptic radio broadcasting ashes through a vendor's
    hair.
I was a bird caught in a church bell,
a machine smothered in attention's grease.

I was the porous stone clanking in the rim of your visor,
but you were the sky whose colors became rigid with memory,
the water that did not part when I entered it,
the mirror whose embrace is final.
Someone served us this pail of slippery wishes before,
and we neither nibbled nor sipped.
Perhaps you're no longer full of burning tires.
Maybe you'll even hear us when we fall.

II

M Is for Mouse and Medicine

The mouse is one of the most ancient medicines used by mankind, and has been in continuous use from very early prehistoric times right up to the present day.

There was a belief in Pliny's time (23–79 AD), which also figures in medieval *Bestiaries*, that the mouse was a spontaneous product of the Nile mud after each inundation. Modern Egyptians, I have been told, also believe in the spontaneous generation of mice from the Nile mud.

In his account of the divine origin of salt, Plutarch suggests this divinity may have arisen because the mineral preserves bodies from decay after the soul has taken flight, and because mice conceive by licking salt.

In his book, *The Ancient Egyptians* (1923), Professor Elliot Smith writes:

> The occasional presence of the remains of mice in the alimentary canals of children, under circumstances which prove the small rodent had been eaten after being skinned, is a discovery of very great interest, for Dr. Netolitzky informs me that the body of the mouse was the last resort of medical practitioners in the East several millennia later as a remedy for children in extremis, as it still is in Europe.

In the Egyptian medical papyri the mouse occurs only three times. In the Ebers Papyrus it figures in a prescription for some sort of rheumatoid trouble "to relax stiffness."

Equal parts of the pig, the mouse, the snake and the cat are to be mixed together and bandaged to the infected part.

A daily ointment made from the fat of the mouse is mixed with that of the lion, hippopotamus, crocodile, donkey, and olive oil.

A hair ointment: Cooked mouse put in fat until it is rotten. Rub into scalp.

In the magical papyrus in Berlin: Make this child, or his mother, eat a cooked mouse. Put the bones around his neck, bound with a string in which seven knots have been tied.

Dioscorides says: It is well known that mice which run about the house can be very useful when cut up and applied to scorpion stings. If children eat them roasted, it helps them stop dribbling from the mouth.

The Algerian physician Abd er-Razzak, who lived at the end of the 17th century, borrowed some of his cures from Dioscorides. In his *Revelation of Enigmas*, which was translated into French in 1874, he offered the following prescriptions:

> When grilled and eaten, the mouse stops dribbling of saliva in children.

> Roasted alive and placed upon the sting of a scorpion, it cures it.

> Applied similarly to splinters and thorns, it draws them out.

The reader who examines Pliny's *Natural History* will find it swarming with mice. The mouse, or parts of it, or its blood or dung appear again and again. The ashes of the head of a mouse, the tail of a mouse, and the entire mouse are used as cures.

For afflicted lungs, African mice, flayed, cooked in oil and salt and eaten will provide relief.

To cure children who cannot hold their water, make them eat cooked mouse.

A Coptic medical papyrus (circa 900–1000 AD) contains this prescription for ulcers: One ounce of wax; two ounces of santal, one ounce of unsalted pig-lard; one ounce of cut-open mouse. Cook and ingest.

In the *Ascent of Olympus* (1692), the author writes: Fried mice are very good to eat. And mice flayed and dried to powder, and the powder mixed with sugar-candy is good for children's coughs. In the *Pharmacopoeia Universalis*, Dr. R. James states: The whole Animal and its Dung are used in Medicine. The Mouse, cut up alive, and applied, draws out Splinters, Darts, and Arrows, and cures the Bites of Scorpions, extracting the poison. The Ashes cure the involuntary flux of the Urine. The Dung purges infants.

Today the mouse is used chiefly for children. It is usually flayed, fried or boiled or made into a pie, and is given to children for incontinence, for uncontrolled dribbling of saliva, and for whooping cough.

It should be noted that in nearly every case the mouse must be skinned or cooked for internal use, and split open for external application.

When a Lancashire mother administers a mouse to her ailing infant, she is doing what mothers living along the banks of the Nile did for their infants six thousand years ago.

Had Gottfried Benn (1886–1957), who served as a doctor in both the First and Second World War, known of the medicinal use of mice, he might have been reminded of a line from his poem, "The Evenings of Certain Lives," and written:

> We begin with mouse pie or powder
> We end as rats' pudding

The use of mice cells in the treatment of certain brain disorders is a recent development.

Some people are afraid that genetic engineers will produce tomatoes containing mice genes.

> "Last
> night I dreamt
> of soft, fried
> mice. Scout's honor."
> William Corbett
> *New & Selected Poems* (1995)

Many psychologists consider a steady diet of television cartoons, particularly if the stories are violent fantasies, to be harmful to a child's social development.

Behind the walls of their offices, Mickey, Minnie, Ignatz and Jerry are gathered around a candle, busy mapping the routes of their next escapade. A tall yellow shadow lurks outside.

74

III

HOLLYWOOD ASIANS

Peter Lorre Improvises Mr. Moto's Monologue

I float outside your windows on rainy nights, a blanket of gray mist you can't peel from the glass. My mechanized eyes are spherical rooms bisected by new dancing knives, irradiated crystal holograms blooming in the brackish pool of winter's shadows. I'm a rug of glistening grit settling on the shelves of atomized fat lodged beneath your epidermal layers. Upgraded teeth pressed closed together. Matching black eyebrows and hair. I'm better than a laboratory frog because I don't need batteries to send my electricity. I lug my skeletal generator around on the slacks of your vacant plots and animal wallets.

Hoist a little red switch, really an eyelid's thin blue vein pulsing an extra drop of thick sweetness, and I begin to twist and bend like tall grass on a spring day. Twitch and quiver on hidden command. I'm a high-end pastoral inmate, an ingratiating drip of diseased music scratching against your fidelity. Deep cranial discharges jettison hot tremors toward the placid surfaces of my deception, that photogenic smile I slide out of my tuxedo pocket like a clean comb. Each little eruption is a hook you can mount a clock or cloud on, I am that free of rust and decay.

Call it a black hole or tunnel sucking me back towards birth. Through the cobbled alleyways of Berlin. Charcoal city smoldering on the frigid Roman plains. Hovel of bunglers and chumps. Ratty fur, bad teeth, cracked hands. Phalanxes clanking rhythmically in the distance. My tantrums are legendary. Hollywood didn't mold me into what I am, a diminuitive silk hurricane approaching America's crafty shores, dapper neon silhouette slipping behind a foil moon, draped bones in a metallic black suit.

Weasel hoofer, bone brain, magpie lamp. I danced past all the tiled tollbooths of Upper and Lower Baby Town. My pointy shoes always slipping neatly into the latest two-step, hip wiggling import, the winding boa line of club searchlights. I invented the toreador horn rack and bongo head romp. Even if the kiss of wet death is the closest I ever got to cozy camera romance, its two car garage and four poster bed, I have more silk gowns and initialed garters than Los Angeles has would-be assassins, swallowed more bullets than martinis. I downed what the fat man couldn't lick with his pleated slipper.

Many times my agent told me I was ready to be a lasso dancer twirling war widows beneath coconut umbrellas, but I didn't like lodge bulbs shining their ties with leather doves. They sat on the glacier below my flood-stained redemption. I may have been the smashed mollusk you nudged aside, a rubber stoolie with a runny nose and thin fingers, or the slimy consonant packs of stubbled ones hunted out of the rubble, but you were the pigeons, fat pillows wallowing in the mire of defeat. Bugs matted down in grease paths of plowed hair. Lard claws scraping warehouse cubicles. It is my voice that seeps through windows, under doormats. I rise through floorboards, leak out of phones, all warm pomade and smooth walking topped by a blazing boutonniere. It's the echo of my lullaby whisper that squeezes the chrome out of chubby limousines. I was one of the few blessed with an insipid whine. I rub long pale digits together, tickle sandy hairs sprouting on moonlit arms.

Morticians wanted to get their boiled forceps on me, shove me into an economy box. They couldn't wait to lug my charred drains out of hotel rooms rented under flowery pseudonyms. Cram me in a bus station locker until a young woman on her way to the lead-lined interior of Philadelphia complains of odors dripping from the metal door next to hers. I was a snotty snot rag, a juicy hobbler, a meal ticket delivered in three languages. I learned to embroider your name perfectly, each letter as sharp and shiny as a new moon on Saturn's horizon. I swallowed the elongated syllables of dusty, broken pills with gusto. A celluloid renegade in possession of all his neurons, a radar dish picking up telepathic wavelengths curdling in the rumpled checkerboards of America's dairy farms. Insidious cackling of righteousness.

I hear your voices clamoring in the layers rubbing against the geological night, mercury tears drifting down tattooed skies. Glottal tubes twisting into gardens. Vibrato of clenched paws pounding red linoleum, demanding the silos be full and straight as the arrows entering General Custer's eyes. I'm one of those arrows. I fly again and again, spin through the wind. My yellow scarf hanging like spit from my chin. You can't disown me because you've never worn out my cashmere coat. I'm an engine of rebuilt fur. I'm what slips through your purified crave.

Peter Lorre Dreams He Is the Third Reincarnation of a Geisha

Opium is the religion of the feeble, the game, and the assaulted. This is a test, soon your fortune teller will be returned to you. Do not switch the dial, you will only activate the storm brewing on the horizon. Black mist drifts in loose bundles across the garden. I have opened the shutters and let in the rain. My poems are seeping into the page, my ragged wings of ink. I want my neck to be licked by a cloud, my eyes to snow. The incense of winter's lengthening shadows leaves it spoon of ashes by my pillow. The tea grows cold. The temple bell is silent, a pile of shoes and limbs growing beside the door. Mount the onyx crutches on the brocade wall, O hill of foolish straw, O devastated dreamer. Come and kneel within the blessed house of mournful music and sip from the trophies of belligerence and belief. Yes, the ruins of an encyclopedia are written in the broken ice of your face. Must you count your tears? Must you fling these classical lamentations into the stream running past your window.

Unable to heal itself, the pond succumbs to the piano of the ancient sky. What do you mean the wind moans like a woman in childbirth? I was a bundle of laundry unfolded at night. I pull my kimono smoking gown tighter. The delicate yellow snakes wrapped around my waist will tattoo your tongue, I promise you that. I must have been screaming through my plastic buttercups this morning. Why else would my vocabulary shift from one pelican to another? Words clustering around dawn's pewter brim. Raw fish sliding down my slashed gullet. I was sure white oxen would come and break the screen separating me from the ones slumped in their plush velvet seats. Withers and liars. Money rubbers with slug bellies, gaping at the raw and the cooked. Rings of smoke rising toward the oculus. Green tea, red macaroni. I was comic relief, suited slime in the background, pinched face in the crowd. You knew me by the slickness of my hair, the shriveled peanut I carried between my manicured teeth.

First I was delicate, a white peony, then I was a shiny delicatessen, something to snuffle over and return. Our leader said I was climbing the ladder of cultural evolution. I took mincing steps, I bowed and shuffled quietly across the rosewood floor, a prized worm. But I didn't mince words, they weren't mine to abuse. My teeth are straight and black in the proper manner. My thighs are long jade mirrors catching the moon's passage from one myth to another, a striped tiger unfurling its blurred banner. Why do you shun me? One of us inhabits a sad drama, the other entertains noisy guests. Don't squawk to me about nobility or honor. I took my raincoat to the dry cleaners, I learned to twirl spaghetti with a knife and spoon. I have something up my sleeve, something other than the arm you would amputate or lick with your leathery tongue. I want that tongue, and someday I shall have it. I am a reflection, a wall you have smeared with feces and blood. When you pluck your eyebrows, are you a chicken strutting through mud? A turtle crossing the road? Basho wrote, the journey itself is the home. And then highways and the theory of eminent domain ousted him from his solitude. My place in history is a mark left on a shirt. I was a waddling pug, and then I was plugged with rubber ballots. I made stone ducks gasp. I was a mulberry leaf the wind tugged loose from a branch, a ginko in a gazebo. My skin glistened on cue in the calculated light. I quivered until the audience mopped their brows with thick fingers. I live in a porous wall of moist projections. I am a dog oozing sweet oil in a butcher shop, a hatless traitor strung up by his heels. Bear claws are a necessary ingedient. Grind the rhinoceros horn to powder, lick the candle wax from your sleeve. Why spawn progeny? why not choose exinction?

Peter Lorre Confesses His Desire To Be a Poet

I've already telephoned Olympus and its legions of winged slaves. Now I'm telling you, as if your ears do function better than the ones glued to the smiling face of our invisible benefactor, our budget conscious director whose velvet folding chair has been stenciled with a thousand and one blessed names. *Platyhelminth, Smorgasbord Snivel, Polar Turpitude.* Names barely whispered in the fetid cannister of our clammy confessionals. Sorry, but I won't kow-tow in the vast illuminated decors of this fissiped carnivorous mammal. I don't want to get my knees dirty, blunt my perfect creases. Sure, I owe the rest stop of my diminishing fame to the dusky shadows coagulating in the pockets of my pristine though misproportioned face, to the serving plate circumference of my bulging eyes, to the superhuman length of my catgut whine, all neatly mounted on a langorous tulip stalk. Sure, I catapaulted over those who snickered whenever I veered before them. But was this my true destiny? Or was it the path along which I ended up drifting like the linden leaves somersaulting in Berlin's purple gutters. India ink seeping into the pools of late October light.

I was an educated snake swaying between night club strolls and yellow backed crawls. A shivering face, a petulant shrug. I was a squirm master. Old cobra, scarred handbag. Call me Maria Mongoose if you must, but what are you? A pustule of fat dumped on a slimy rock? Some lint that strayed into my custom cuffs? I performed the lead in *Waltz of the Seven Fears*, and I threaded hallway unions of stunted shadows, little grunts gripping their hand saws, hammers sprouting from their ingrown feet.

After I became a citizen, these were my options. Be a giant among shrimps or a dwarf among giants. I was a refugee squeezed by the blossoms of a wet clamp, and I became a sinister grope encased in sweet dollops of rotting steam, a pillow to drag a whip across on poker night. Like a violin, I trembled sweetly at the sight of manufactured pain.

Oh Mister Ping Pong, they used to whisper on the lot, you dropped your swollen left tennis ball, your tattooed ostrich egg, your glass fly. But I swirled past their prickly couch, and their flaccid insinuations, a sleepy pyromaniac drenched in pink clouds of seashell powder. Their coats of cellar breath and gilded flatulence didn't stick to my limousine. My advantage, a bullfrog's thick lids and slow blink. In those midwestern towns flopped beside the tracks, like a dirty tablecloth, I could pass as one of the new streetlights, a sentinel working when no one is looking. I get paid to wrap fur and silk around my oozing surfaces, to insult the puffy meringues of intelligence pitched in their seats. And when the shadows shift, and the light settles on another face, more handome than mine, you can rest assured that my cactus tongue is busy slithering down a naked throat.

I pen these modest invasions, these veiled valentines, at night, when the moon is a tall cold candle, a steady flame in the dark hills of Hollywood's dust bowls. I wanted to shed my whine and become words vibrating in the folds of your brain. I need to know in which bungalow I will finally take shape. To what island of lost trials am I condemned? Or was I nothing more than a porcine spoon stirring planks of mud, a porcelain porkchop draped over a fleur-de-lis scarf? Is that it? Was I just another tuxedo cruising the shallows of clubbed waters? Another sack of flounders dropped onto an embossed plate?

Like bad honey, my girth slowly thickened in the camera's embrace. But I didn't become a bulbous hulk drifting sideways across the knives of a sunlit bay. I was easily disposable, a gagged rope stuffed in the pleated boot of a sleek sedan. I was something you had to get rid of over and over again, an infected penny clinging to the grooves of your sweaty palms, a nickname that followed you out of the groves of childhood.

Fedoras are for fat *federales* and homely hombres. Stamped out in a sweat shop, my slim perfumed doll comes in a leather carrying case. Custom accessories include alligator pumps and a snubnose gat. Engraved pearl handle, smooth and warm in your hand. Another box functions as my wardrobe, its ebony doors inset with tight mirrors and soft even light. I am a trophy of small, perfected steps and pleading impulses.

I whined and I winced, a beaver lined rag sopping up fried puddles and popcorn guffaws. I pleaded for mercy and more. But my fans didn't become radios. They didn't replay my monologs, full of flittering and fluttering. Their clodhopper noggins tuned to smaller wavelengths, mesh they could sink their tin stars into. To them, I was nothing more than an ornate doorway through which strangled vowels and stomped consonants spilled their sweat, a geiger counter registering the tremors of those who surrounded me. But I knew better. I was pure contempt grinning feebly inside my trade mark. Spoof or spout, I am living proof of an obsolete equation, that all bricks are squeezed from the dust of popular sequels. This brick knows no building you would enter.

Peter Lorre Wonders Which Artist
Should Paint His Portrait

Case stockings shutters gum smoke lampshade shoes. Tall lace plunge and a stout guzzler with a short muzzle. Long black sapphire sedans careening against a chorus of bubbles. Candle background of lodge fixtures, fur trophies, and carbon lumps. Unshaven gray moon pronged above obsidian streets, cellars full of canceled leather. Chrome stars welded to the spokes of tenement nights. Glacial soap monuments, palm heels soft against ashen cheeks.

All I could yield was this face. It was my spigot, my sword, and my shadow. Tarnish followed me everywhere. A bleached doll's head twisted off at the neck, a klaxon brain's bristling aquarium amplified through a window's rheumy membrane. Beady black eyes. The kind you see in stuffed squirrels, a dusty acorn clutched in cobwebbed paws. Forever was the rage that year. O to be mounted on the toothy pedestal of sweet taxidermy. O to be embalmed in the camera's glowing formaldehyde. I was pluck lucky. I was ignited in the prism halls.

On the outside lanes I heard heads swiveling when I passed. The mirror's salts ransomed to the highest ankle. I was slime in a neatly pressed cheroot, pyramid smoke rising from my ringed head. I was the silk boxer shorts of volcanic leers, something clean and dirty, untouchable and fascinating. Oklahoma swooners wanted to grab my face with the pliers of dirt trickling from their lips.

I want to be another stumble of flesh glimpsed from a crack in the arcade's nougat facade. Can you see me without remembering my trimmed voice boiling in the cauldrons of rural drive-ins? old cars quivering to a fresh line of mattresses ticking in the calcified vortex of gingham's faded dark. Scuffed kneecap hand clamp refusals. Derelict promises, unbuttoned scratches, and sprawled whimpers. Parish fandangos perishing before mainspring purdahs.

A dented hubcap, a hoisted scalp, a tuxedo towel wheeled through a sieve of hoops. This laminated stem, that molasses skeleton. Pummeled slop poured into a briefcase jug. Lacquered lackey with a slight tin verb. You know them all by their fame, their loss of glass proximity. These are the citizens whose matching hands are preserved in the corruptions of pearl cement, lost gallopers strapped to a bicycle of dimes. I was fresh from the ancient sewers of Berlin when I joined the army of fish flopping toward the western citadel of cooling shores. O Island of Lost Ghouls, we chimed, you are the Ohio over-ture of our fatal dreams.

Inside your propane studio, its slate straps and northern light, a ravaged acne mop licks the vomit off your claws. I squeeze the ointment out of coy poodles, you muddle across the pores in boots of oil soak. A clock erases sod details rusting in the roars of our stiff rising.

Phonograph daylight warps any chance for us to strike a splashy tune. Autograph clowns adjust their portable noses, hammer down their electric ties, raise the shades of their put-tied hems. The mold of a famished spire burns in me still, its tarred finger pointing toward the owl eye night. I want to scrape down these trays of crab slivers and molten crumbs, leave the ants to the rocks where they dance and pray.

Can you lend me the shaping iron of your frayed stump? Or offer me a slab of cold soliloquy in paint's blackened tongue? Not ham on immaculate dread, I've licked that stoop before.

Will I ever become the residue of your mature simplicity? I want the sludge to harden into a circular map of my inside skin, the one whose face of inconsistencies never debuts on the silver screen. Will this feral drain ever be gathered into a crust of intimate incandescence? Suspended and finally let loose?

Peter Lorre Prepares for His Final Soliloquy

There isn't time to measure the plunge of winter's corpse or trace the height of stacked shadows beckoning me to enter their tunnels of calcium ascending a blue ladder. Sides of wind shift their faces forward to the glass. Handles moisten the rims of their bright lips. A siphon clamp, I scrape pebbles from the horns of my face, shake off flecks of mottled soil.

Standard frills in the rhyme of temporary brightness. The angel draped in his cloak of red medals and strong oaths was wrong when he whispered: These few moments will be the keystone to your character. What gnawing tonic spilled through this feathered suede, this fur snail? I was always a belted overcoat puckered by a solid umbrella, the one with a runny voice and pickled lids. Nothing about me hangs sharp in the molten evening air, supported by two long thick arms of pink granite, except perhaps the farm of my dirty head and the two sounds only I know how to rub together.

Caterwaul crescendo. I return to my appointed task of turning the water wheel, its call descending in nine half-tones with a great crevice formed by the fifth. Sometimes I use a rhinoceros whip, other times a tape measure woven from buzzard feathers. An oil can clangs against the counting post glowing amidst last season's lava. Pillow honks shake my knitted cap. Like England, Hollywood has its "Lake Country" and it lies in the valley just beyond the archeological museum where the first significant specimens remain on executive display. Crunchy bogus and log slop. A cathode diet of donut soap.

The nearest pockets of fresh air, shady stands of trees and pools of cumulus quiet, are to be found on one of the traffic islands monitoring the motor flow between hills and shore, its blanket of glittering fish. How am I to climb above the shingled roof of yesterday's voices? To your supernal delight, my own voice laughs at me when I am most eloquent about the injuries my body must absorb. Donkey sponge waddling across the boards. Thud cloth striping the floor. Vestiges are visible whenever I pass the algae of a Roman mirror or stand in a garage full of mementoes and creased sunlight. O sod phaeton, I tried building a bridge to the postcard where I started out, a circular green park full of chrome plated baby strollers and heavy set women gathered like baled hay beneath starched conical hats. I inflated clouds with rows of ochre, golden yellow, and red arrows. I twisted my cascading curls and pissed in my bonnet. Someone's lips left a folding scar burning through my tongue.

Insect match in the sprockets of memory's tornado sag. Crumbling arcades, more rust rising through the stains. Spine flaps down. Bandaged decimals. Lapidary drone in the leaves of the buzzed house. I must hurry before the old man draws the curtains shut, and the audience is left without a reason to applaud my imminent departure. Swindled pride. There was a time when I was a sedan chair on which other men puffed their pigeon chests, like calendars of kettle powder and icy smoke. Amber apricot faces pinched by fronds of artificial light. Who wants to linger by the list of ashes numbered in the basement? Who wants to measure the weight of cash strapped to my slithering howl? What about the episode chambers no one dares mention over martinis? The gift wind sweat? The shiver greetings of the skull market?

The red-eyed bat of my cutlass circles the naked bulb of my droopy brawn. Old bug loon. Saddle breath and stars of tarred ice. Twitchy shell. Bulging socket shrug. I was doodled on by the itch of others. Well heeled on the outside, I healed well on the inside. Spent curses bubbling between my sausage teeth. Fat slide drying on a wall, white and plain and thick in the merciless heat of history. I was a parlor athlete caught in a yawn. A civil idiot. A junior messenger.

Who dances now among the serrated edges of scattered rain? Who wantonly drinks the last drops of cold green soup? Who breaks a dish so that each member can carry a piece home? Who counts the peonies lifting their red dresses to the tongues of a tilting wind?

Tell them all, I've gone out to the platform to wait
for an octopus moon to hoist me
to the brimming balconies of a yellow heaven.

Genghis Chan: Private Eye XXI

I am a hat softener
in the trade confession

a belly down carpet stamp
Jerks are my toys

I spray them
with my battering ham

over easy side order
flies to grow

Slime covers us tall
Flags flow meaner

on the other tide
Puddle around with stack beans

Slab the spotted pig
before he drivels

This grind of activity
flavors the rest

First muskets and mouse caps
Then caskets and caboose taps

Lotion drains down
your past leaves

burns the flock
back to one

These are the rodents
you oil in your tree

the heads you snip off
at the wreck

When gum plays to spoon
tide of the mouth

You have to screech
around your powdered baby elf

Tune your acne clumps
to the smallest dimes

Genghis Chan: Private Eye XXII

Aquarium night steers
two intersected occupants

(a motel I and the one
inside its vowel remnant)

toward a library of ledges
Stack doodle know-how

and lake metal shivers
A frigid stare card

I or my tongue
am the lizard

who bakes
your last animal residue

A tropical fossil haze
in an empty

farmhouse suit
Potion cogs

distributed beneath
the neural

carport
A limousine

transmission
aerialist

sparkling
stewed spew

on the pyramid floor
I or the one

curled around
my voice

celebrate the humid glow
of another radius

burning the staircase of
its insect logic

Genghis Chan: Private Eye XXIII
(Haiku Logbook)

1.

Feed him his lights
Poke down wallet sniffer
Probe hoisted tar dispute

2.

Silk crave
Worn buckles slipped tight
Crawl on tide rock

3.

Linger and blunder
Slave dunks cooking for pearls
Failed to let dust control his fur spree

4.

School pigeon hot in rack
Circus hat moth fear
Leaf gnasher in girdle triumph

5.

Toasted of his wooden thighs
Flight ladles yearning their slicks
Empty star on a valley sheet

6.

Could feel the flute in his glands
Young wild sputtering into his cursed zone
Savage hex in retail lobby

7.

Investigate domestic squirrel
Donkey liner puddling his horse
Horizontal rain delay

8.

Idaho rooster fed in wooden slipper
Slack addict combing in hunk yard
Bend fools around calloused dumb

9.

Spilled his ruts over sawdust shore
Slow knots disturb gym lass
Lunch his flights out

10.

Flies never lie
Sediment selection trail
Ride behind trick stall

11.

Snow looter in a feathered gab
Nuzzling pansy growler
Loot to spill

12.

Scalding dump steer
Oiling the wool
Slump diner over boulder

13.

Burden of fruit calls upon you
Stumps from an abandoned reject
Spud dude in rotten candy stains

14.

Corner blasted door owner
Rents out of cape
Lust burns to act residential

15.

Tells child for seeded monkey
Curtain praiser
In the wine of fire

16.

Stare of lookers grabbed by strife
Face high flood rakes mall
Shark storage crank

17.

Cloud agency floats belly cup
Dish crosser unlegged by can
Thigh lotion signals make-up fall

18.

Lust whim for rope
Born to bruise
Pixie crate

19.

Leather glass border
Fed on treat rustler
Scalawag sound unit

20.

Grime scavenger
Branch of cotton posed skids
Spore another wit

21.

Bound in rusty hotel broom
Turn the key and kit brighter
Whittled sighs almost paved him

22.

Potion score drifts through pails
Little piles of dirty honey
Slick to climb over incoming raves

23.

Plum ox bashed lead
Wig coiler thrashed to sound
Cost soggy toy scout route

24.

Traffic cram in funnel
Tithe trace in milk bandage
Muscle can stoves the hunch

25.

Two cheek bonus spray
Ground runaway style
Bout of order

26.

Retain bottom robot impresario
Lease placate room
Exhibition kiss

27.

Revisits drapery in a winch
Scrambled the sea quencher
Short groom drama flays the spare

28.

Plover and gout
Unretaintable lotion quickness
Vile under

29.

Bank clobber miss lap
Spotted race crack lasher
Earned his graft

30.

Returned gift plodder
Tall signs
Point to sudden breath

Genghis Chan: Private Eye XXIV

Grab some
Grub sum

Sub gum
machine stun

Treat pork
pig feet

On floor
all fours

Train cow
chow lane

Dice played
trade spice

Makes fist
first steps

Genghis Chan: Private Eye XXV

Dimple sample
Rump stump

Dump fun
Dim sum

Slum rubble
Gong sob

Strong song
Oolong

Rinky dink
Trinket rock

Duck walk
talk muck

Genghis Chan: Private Eye XXVI

Honking
Hong Kong

Road map
Toad face

Hong king
"store lord"

Dead cold
Unload

Old gold
Smoke gripe

Fan stamp
Dance step

Stamp fan
Sampan

Gunk junk
Lug wretch

Wrench nut
Cut stench

Genghis Chan: Private Eye XXVII

Moo goo
Milk mush

Guy pan
Piss pot

Genghis Chan: Private Eye XXVIII

Droll moll
Cool doll

Shark stamp
Park bunch

Key chain
Chin key

Sly jive
Yell high

IV

Mon Alias, Mona Lisa

1.

Mon Alias
Osma Nila
Nasal Moi
Aims Loan

Lois Nama
Ia Salmon
Salam Ion
Asa Limon

2.

Maison Al
Oils Amna
No Salami
Ails Noma

Limo Sana
Ilsa Mano
Siam Nola
Alamo Sin

3.

Mia Salon
Omni Alas
Noa Islam
Ala Simon

Los Anima
Isla Omna
Soil Mana
Al Simona

4.

Moli Nasa
Oana Slim
Nils Amoa
Amil Sona

Losa Mina
Isam Anol
Soma Nail
Aman Silo

5.

Moan Sail
Oman Sila
Noli Masa
Asim Olan

Lom Siana
Isa Nomal
So Manali
Ana Moils

6.

Manila Os
Osam Anil
Nosa Mail
Ali Nomas

Lion Asam
Ian Sloma
Soli Maan
Alisa Mno

7.

Masa Nilo
Olim Anas
Nilo Sama
Amin Oals

Lina Mosa
Inam Osal
Samo Anil
Almi Snoa

8.

Milo Asna
Olna Misa
Nols Amia
Alo Isman

Loin Asma
Ismal Ona
Snail Moa
Alms Noia

9.

Misa Lona
Onas Mila
Naso Lima
Asno Amli

Lias Noam
Isal Onam
Salo Nami
Alon Amis

V

Angel Atrapado XIX

I was the toad in tinsel,
you were the donkey in red suede.
We were grape lollipops
dawdling on the porch of moon's swollen tongue,
its dustpan open to a dirty sky.
We had missed our exit, and were slipping deeper
into a room of burning books
folding their yellow wings around us.

Yes, I heard the ones linked to the hallways
behind my eyes, those little red tubes full of saliva.

Yes, I heard a voice or thought back there say:
You can tell yourself this story
if you think it will guide you.
You can go on writing these words down,
as if they were steam.

Yes, I still count the sleeves missing from your best shirt.
Yes, I still carry the remaining buttons, those pearl snails,
    in my mouth.
But this was not what I haunted,
this faded blue gown dangling in the middle of a sunlit room,
white flowers resting in every corner.
It was not even where I was when my eyes were open,
    like torn envelopes,
but it was where I flew,
and what I did when you were standing,
pants punched up around your wrinkles.
Those songs still catch me in their trembling tines.

These days, everywhere I row, I see myself in the canvas
I did not paint, the one I am selling.

I am down in the grease, my puddles of milk
folded through a dollar and a leash.
I am an apparatus of some sort,
wadded tissue stuffed in every vent.

I told him: Some horses have three lips,
but only one of them works.

I told him: Keep your little wall rocket
in my summer safe.

I told him: Heat the coal and forget the tent.
There is a leak in this chair you will never get to frost.

Fresh batteries started transmitting their messages
through last remnants of yesterday's sky,
its beaded carpet of inexpensive noise.
I am sifting through the aftermath,
rows of chipped cells glued to the call.
Yes, I wanted to be there, wanted to be inside the hills
leading back to your voice,
the one that warned or scorned me,
the one I stole from the loading dock,
the reddening rock of reptile appearances.

Someone said: Can you stave the flight?
Someone whispered: Can you enslave the bright?

I was a place for hands to rummage.
A four door garage sale, all my unclad pajamas on display.
A row of polished medals dangling from the crests
of those I never clutched. A chorus line of wooden pegs.
Twirl of magazine stances and ceiling rates.

116

Smell of plots thickening in the map.

Broken glass blooms in the rind.

Sunlight lingers at the bottom of the lair.

Another cabin roars toward the pyre.

Angel Atrapado XX

One of us is about to get up and dance in the dark,
one of us is about to roll over and spit into the pillow.
Or is it that one of us is about to tilt the beaker,
and one of us is about to sift through the pollen.
Those clothes again, the ones you seldom wear,
the ones your friends greet
when you meet them on the trickle of stairs.

Another voice begins: I knew that
when I stepped through the door
I would suddenly be visible,
that there would be nothing left to hide,
that even my tongue was going to be inspected by the hands
I brought them, fresh pliers from the Museum of Forbidden
    Tastes.

Another voice takes up where this one has faded: Each verb
will be returned to you when you have nothing left to pair.
This is the outside you will never leave,
a telephone booth filled with sounds of smoke and water.

The voice who whispers in the moonlit parking lot:
Once we did it beside another couple, but when they asked us
to move to the front, to be alone on that mound of hyenas,
to be the only contents of the game, I slid through the
    window.
Later, I could see myself on the other side,
my body was being held in the air, like a fork or a plate,
and someone was collecting the juices dripping off the bones.

I wanted to hawk your dress, but I wanted to keep
its leather scraps between my teeth.
I wanted to carry it to you,
but I wanted to throw it at your feet.

There is no middle sound where the notes
coat the sunlit leaves.
One either pays the mud or frays the air.
And then it is time to trade in those rides again,
collect the stamps you need for a new set of teeth,
blue ones this time, blue as the day you were born.

The plastic brain still ticking, rubber paws
spinning around the ceiling fan, its rusted slats.
Lying in bed and staring into the funnel
rising from the moonlight's forehead.

Sod does not forgive those who repeat themselves, she said.
There is a moment when the head flops forward and the
        tongue
extends its rails between my sapphire tears.
The wind comes back, bringing the slag we wore
when our accusations churned with delight.

Something squashed in the palm.
Old medicine crystals,
their yellow gas strapped in glamor.
I was diagramming the remaining illusions
we had to penetrate, their ventral elongations
shifting shadows through the computer's remaining saliva
        ducts.
I was a machine introducing myself to a machine,
and it was sending its signals directly through me,
because I was not the I it wanted, but the one
who had been programmed to float between.

Pooch or mutt, what matter this leash,
said the one in the dog suit,
the one who had whammo on the mind.

Angel Atrapado XXI

Something slips between
Someone's slip or lip

The one whose mouth is a cloud.

The one who says: I cannot be here
without seeing you there, doing that now.
Then always on its way. And me,
this knot of nothings cast aside,
nowhere among the onrush of sounds.

The one who stays inside and says:
Because I am always there, completing the story
in which I am erased, a bothersome blip on a blue screen.

And the one who whispers into the ear of these voices:
This is the bridge of remote control eyes,
luminous cilia carpeting night's littered parking lot.
This is the car in which we will never meet,
the one whose name is stamped in charcoal and snow.
And, yes, this is where I am grinding my skin
in the satchel of sand you gave me.
And, no, I have not started doing
what you expected, bleeding from the sleeves
or tying my hands to the clock above the bed.

The one who says: Today, the how and why applications
will be denied. The windows are on fire,
and the ladders are melting in the rain.

The one who says: Wrong code, wrong abode.
This *this* empty even of me.
I cannot enter any lair that leads to you,
warm tunnels of trim fiascos and spotted slants,
for I am the window through which you see yourself
     walking away.

The one who says: I begin to smolder, I begin to shoulder.
Or I have started to stare, I have started to flare.

Upper and lower levels of attention.
Aquamarine trembling beneath summer's cumulus residence.
I hear myself talking to the one who sits inside me,
the one who leaks gasoline onto the carpet
where I stand, the one who holds a hammer behind the eyes.
Perhaps you shall step forward and be squeezed cold.
Perhaps the one you think you are speaking to
has never been there, that the voice you hear
is either an insinuation or a mirage,
a flower or a garage where you park your favorite flaws,
the little ones eating their way up the vine.

The one who says: You have fallen
into the voices circling the rooms inside you,
the one where you hid and the one where you were found.
Remember, you are nothing more than an oversized suitcase
whose mouth is locked in snow.

The one who says: I hear this spoken at the edge of false
     repair.

The one who says: Words are gangplanks waiting at every
     corner.

The one who whispers: A little clump or a whittled jump.
The window is open, and the clouds are free for the baking.

122

One learns not to be afraid of the slights.

There is thinking to do, he says, but does not speak.

The one who points: A heap of bread makes the best lapse of
    all.

Tour the crusts between this and this, now and now.
Beat the dust you have always wanted to lap.

Who does one hear in the voices
between the words you try to fling together?
What words never become the forms they point to?
The ones slipping through the grains of what was said
beside our displays? Or the ones that never rise
to the surface of what is being said?

Or is it the one who says: Resume consumption at tall costs.
The chlorophyll recess is nearly over.

Talk and listen
Stalk and glisten

This tongue is a flower. Someday you will hear what it has
    to pay.

Angel Atrapado XXII
(The Elements)

The one who says:
I did not cross the line you drew in the air.
I did not stoop to steal the air you buried in the sand.
Had you known it was yours, you might have used it.
Had I known it was mine, I might have saved it.

Someone is speaking into a tape recorder,
someone with a name that sounds like yours,
someone who claims she (or perhaps he) dreamed
that they (there must have been two of them) were you,
that they had your hair and hands,
saw through your eyes, and did the things they did
to someone else, someone with the names you wanted for
    your own.

The voice that says:
This is my story, it is the only one,
and the ones who are in it
will never leave the rooms I have erected
around their trails of rust.

The one who says:
This is the name of the wind
that took us through the story that was not yours to tell,
the one that held us up to the sun, the one
that documented the yearning, the burning, of our hair,
the clench and stench of our flesh.

The one who says:

I want to penetrate
the planes of smoke between you and your mouth,
I want to steal the earthen jar,
where you store your bones,
the ones you use to beat
sunlight into metal,
moonlight into stone.

The one who answers before you begin:
The woman you are looking for is a man,
and that man is a name. It is the name of the door
between you and the tongue you borrowed
from the mouth of the one who is dead,
the one whose head is mounted on the pillow beside you.
The head which whispers the name you cannot utter,
the name you are called by when you are alone in your room
and no one is listening, and the hand moving above the pages
resembles a turtle dragging its burning house toward the sea.

The one who stammers:
I lie down beside her dress and cry.

The one who answers:
Now that you have collected your tears
in crystal vials, what will you say to the rainbows of light
and their wet walls arching across your desk?
What will you write on the inside of your tarnished sighs?

The one who announces:
You will not lift my dress over my head,
you will not wear my shirt and shoes.
You will not point that camera at me,
you will not see me with someone else doing
something that has no name.

The one who answers back:

When will you take off these buttons
and swallow them like pills?
When will you fill the room
with shoelaces of seaweed and salt?

Angel Atrapado XXIII

The team of little blue voices began storming
through the dream trust collecting in their pockets,
looking for the lining where they had been hidden.
The rented mouth that kept them from speaking,
and the tainted mouth that covered them
with rows of candy kisses.

I thought it was over, one of them said.
The one with star tissue covering his crests.
The one with handles rising toward a perfect smile.
I thought I had reached the point where there was no picture
on the wall, no window to look through,
no air squeezing the room with dust.
I thought I was in that place
where the lines of the story never reached me.

You are the guest, I am the turtle.
We fit inside each other
like pebbles in a worm,
a worm in dirt.
She sat down and started to draw a picture of us,
while I began pacing in front and to the side of her,
whittling a picture of a word.

Yes means *maybe*, and *maybe* means *no*.

It was where we were when I placed your hand
between my prune colored flies, the zone of try and taste
what your tongue cannot clutch.
You are the buffer or buffet,

the butler whose feet I nailed to the floor.

Sometimes I want to laugh,
a big laugh,
big enough to be a door.
Here is the door, I will say.
It has no handle, and the wing
you are looking for
has long since been buried in another direction.
Other times I want to feel you crying
so that I can fill you once again with water
I siphon from the well I keep locked in my closet,
the secret well where I bathe each morning
before cutting back the remnants of my stolen face.

When I abandoned the piston, you were left floating in your
     hair.
A torn sheet hovering above an empty yield.

I am the glass whose rim
you will never touch,
the shimmering column of air
you passed through
in an attempt to pierce my reflection.

I can't be with two of you.
One is too much.
If I was with both sides,
I would always be waiting for one voice
to hear the other.

She told him she met someone and was moving in with him.
She had waited long enough, perhaps too long.
If she waited any longer she would be buried in her apron,
the one they stained the morning they never left the kitchen,
the one she lifted to her face each time she lied to the dishes.

The one who says: I was lying in the park and waiting.
I kept licking all my stingers and running them
along the signs leading to your diary.

I wanted your hands to tie me open,
ride me down like a book whose bruises are burning.

Angel Atrapado XXIV

It was early October,
a time of gathering insect husks
floating on the pools of sleep.
We were in an adjacent room,
licking the last of summer's slime from our fur,
a basket of roses wedged between our teeth.

You were going to be the sweetened gum of something more one
      day.
Once you could, a whiff of a chance, but now never is always.

I'm the dotted line where someone stamps a name.
This is what you sold me: fountain of crusts,
fading glimmer, birds pecking at corpses,
their frozen cries.

Horizon's rented curtain and the city of yellowed stars
      that lies beyond.
The rails of thinning voices to which this is addressed
are being erected out of what you remember,
drone of declarations and rags of blue rust.

Intersecting backgrounds
rearrange their cones and vectors.
Planes tilt, accumulated orders
spill out of their contours.
Vines of urchin syllables begin spreading
through the Cartesian nervous system.
A way of making yourself small takes over:
Slow roast of dripping surges.

Ledges of venom crashing down and up.
Another insistence felt
in the mesh of the many you cart.

Perfection's violet plume and the inevitable plummet,
immovable dome of flies and the stalls
on which rosy warnings are branded.
Why go back to what you cannot leave?
Crackling voices, burning rungs.
Voices made of wood and voices made of water,
the ground rotting between their varnished clamps.

Am I always to be here among them?
Bruised tongue wilting on a spine.
City where the dead line up and vote.

I was carrying your dress to the window,
I was watching your shoes float in fire.

One of the ones whose air we never sift
                              pointed.
These are our silhouettes,
the ones we learn to bury in the swirls of
our necessary representations and lashed economy.
We will boil a nectar of glue,
              a sweet tonic
we can use to write on each other's lungs.

The lax within. I was folding a spear
around the ledge of my forehead,
and I was running toward the door.

I was looking for the one who said:
This you is not you.
I was looking for the one whose voices
leave me where I am:

In the shattered mirror of stars.

I'm holding my head in my hands,
a green sponge dripping with style.
I'm posing for a copy of *The Stinker*
by August Rodent, a bronze spatula
whose imitations are scraped throughout the lair.

Angel Atrapado XXV

I was starting to boil
the last of the glasses we once shared
when you broke back: There is nothing to steer at.

Was I the only one in this world, our words,
its prehensile corridors and bleached doom,
who was full of embers and ooze?
The talking zombie with the small and empty hat?
The newly elected assayer in a village of vicious morons?
Or was I the grim pester? the prim jester?
the last bubble of a terminated squirt?

More speckled daubs
are trickling into the sluices of my crumpled veneer,
its pulmonary drains of twisted slogging.
Someone is leaking words
into the silver rivers of a mirror or mirage,
what I hold up before the memory capsule of my enameled
        visor
so that I might finally feel that I'm completed
without being complete, a bridge floating
in deregulated space.
If only for the moan of a moment.

There are always two or more
to be glued down by.

Another winged feature sputtering
in the web of moon's pilfered lace.

There is a winter that can never be drummed back into a lake,
a row of pronouns that cannot be assigned to elemental desks,
a blackboard full of volcanic rhomboids.

You said: I will not characterize you
if you do not try try to bake me
into a grappled lie, a furry spout
poking into the salted envelopes of a city's spine.

You said: I cannot repeat
what you never said to me.
The entrance to the radiator is lined with specks.
All the ladders have been lifted through the clouds
and there is neither a *where* nor a *what* on which to land.

Yes, the ground on which we talk grumbles.
No, I do not hear it.

You said: I washed my rungs of trampled grab,
I became a wooden sled
fans used to reach the bottom of a pleated spill.
I was the tree that waited for them,
I was the throttle full of noisy questions.

You said: I'm waiting for the voices
inside me to reside. Someday
you shall hear them talking beside the body
you think is yours, the one you visit
when you are alone,
its throne full of velveteen soup.

You said: The I and the you
have been set on pyres.
We hold the latches that will praise them
with leaps of smoke.

Or is it this me who has been speaking all along?
The one that was shorn of its body.
A lightbulb with neither a tongue nor a shadow,
something shining from the folds of a captured tie.

One day there is a wall of mud surrounding the city,
something each of us enters and from which we never emerge.
A gathering of wilted particles inside a fleshy scheme.
A voice flies out of the damp skin surrounding you:
Is this because both the mud and I can be squeezed between
      bricks?
Or have I been stalking the wrong doors of myself all along,
thinking the one who is talking will finally make me loam?.

Yes, one of the voices that is mine says, this sheet is on loan.
And all the objects on it are made from a comet's dirty water.
Had I thrown them in the yields of today I would have
      said so.

Angel Atrapado XXVI
(Dear Rilke)

Who among the many I am would answer me if I stalled out?
That's why I tried to pave the voice of my stolen elf,
later,
after we told ourselves and each other
there was a document declaring
we had never been there, in the room
with the bed of mud and leather,
tattooed stowaways on a swiveled saddle
facing away from the stars pinned to the wall.

This, I wanted to say, was a story I made up
but then I would be flying through my teeth.

A wilted butterfly stuck to a stenciled pail,
the wind's hearse infiltrating the pockets of our sweaters,
the ones we knitted out of children's hair.
It is not my name I must repeat, but the shame of it.
Did you remember to light the pyre?
watch the smoke rise through
the broken windows of my borrowed eyes?
If I told you once, then I never told you.
We were praying again; and,
like all the other times we prayed,
the words never penetrated the page,
reached the horizon glowing beyond our lies.
Do you like to watch me leave myself behind?
on the chair where you place
a glass of wine, an axe, and a candle?
Will you catch me and stuff me

full of wooden charms?

Which one of you will unbutton
the swelling that fills my mouth?
I am a sponge floating
on a hedge of blue crusts,
and you are a linoleum tile
stamped with sharp yellow roses.

Can you help me slither across the garage?

I am the path a fly takes
in order to reach the tornado.
I am a photograph registering
the seismic interferences
rising through your hands,
their gloves of poisoned meat.
Each of us is a service entrance
made of candied shoes, a toehold
filled with imitation juice.
Perhaps by tonight one of us
will begin stirring the swill
until it swells
the withering within.
We must learn to adjust
to the ruts and rows,
make glue out of the bones
we shed each summer.
I prefer leftover steam
and teeth stolen from a dog.
I prefer to be left where I am,
but I do not know the name of this place,
only that it sails through me.
I am a window through which you see a landscape—
green blue flames rising toward the wind's coiled throat.

VI

FORBIDDEN ENTRIES

Forbidden Entries I

She is sleeping in the clasp of her sapphire pond while she unbuttons another string of leaves between her moat and rungs. Plastic earphone brigades sweep the vaults. I am standing in a corner, painting concentric circles with the wooden clump growing from my mouth. Foam clamps the canvas to its coffee cans. Red and green silk wires snake across her classical pose, circle the floor, and enter the story I am transmitting to her buried diary, its stages of fluctuation.

He writes: I went there to be washed, my body immersed in fluids dripping from glass pipes and blackened wooden jars, the ones that hold the mouth down and the ones that the mouth releases from its nacreous piles, blue watches glowing behind facial replacement screens. Electronically programmed organ insertion. Laws of the feed written on every perfumed stall.

He writes: I went there to be sifted out of the sand collecting in my shoes, to become a stake of soap slipping into her wrinkled skirt, its yellow tapestry and green hunting cogs. I went there to have my hands tied behind my mask, its pink shed and velvet distress. I sneaked across the bridge dividing the city into upper and lower legions. I walked past houses full of postponements on display, past houses tilting toward the waves of their recital pyres, past houses pulled from the waters of ancient hair, its wet acquittals.

He writes: There is a river that neither starts nor ends, a window or door rising from its pail of ink and blue smoke.

He writes: She is steering a delirious swig when I enter her final closet and lay next to the mirror turned to the wall.

Dear Lower Lid or Fast Minute On Earth, Dear Throbbing Crest or Sobbing Best, I have been unable to form either the syllables of my crescent flame or to remember what I called you ever since I tripped open my skull.

Milk spurts down borrowed lies. You do not answer the question: Does she sway beneath the striped thorax of her toy? I always read the books my father hid beneath his willow, glide of stained pose soaking through packaged feathers. I inserted stolen hours between flicked covers, pictures outlining possible grips one could imitate in the damp stark. Clouds and tranquilizers marked the first and last lap. Old expressions became a convenience one could slip on. Looking over her shoulder or mine, cooking back and winking. Her sponge floats between tong slender legs. Massive verbs light up a blouse, its bell of torn decay. She links his rented stingers, smiles written all over her journal grin.

He writes: I carefully lifted the motions of each scent, waited for more contours to press against my curled lamp. Signals flared up, bells stringing my ears to bed's hard sound. Difficult to monitor the sources of all incoming pulses, their ruby shimmer. I spoke up wet and planted my car on the windowsill. Finger stints tried kissing on fires turning in ant hill sprain. I was a pimply crag cooking in mirrors. A limbless ladder rising from the mire, a storm walker pressing through muddy picnic sounds, a gunshot jelly jar slithering up the aisles of the school tray. I clocked home pioneers climbing the fountain.

These are the best rhymes of your strife, my father stormed. These are the days you will never pay off, the burlap you will never drift. I watched him return to the woodwork and crammed more pages into hours. I waited for the new radiator wiggles to bump against my ramp.

I began as a laundry silhouette coating the vines above a dented square. I was standing in a lizard arcade, dotted spines intersecting satin cleats, their sticky tongues. The puppet circumference was still spreading through the blush of optical relay stations. Stuffed palms sanding my itchy mirror. I started to stab the little insects of my growth, their motel fuzz, make them tumble from their marble sedan.

I began burning my shoes and clocks, everything that exposed me to my willingness to be there. He wanted more than a trail of his ripped wanting. Lesson one: Nurse his lies. Learn to sleep in a casket of day old dread. Finally, I told him what he wanted to hear, my nylons stinging the lip of his giddy astronaut skull, its frozen fragrance and broken smile. It isn't a ticket to grovel. It isn't a ticket to give. And then: Clot this trace before he returns to live, a petal of sand brushing against my gauze plug.

Forbidden Entries II

A fling sized bed slips onto the balcony of a picture frame motel, newly pressed mold of different colored arms and legs extending from beneath wave of daisy lint sheets. Overturned lava lamp, green and red balloons undulating in factory issue teardrops. Shiny blue pajamas stuck to plaster swirls. A tongue without discernible flavor imbedded in the pillow beside them. *Who left it here and why?*

The first whisper, followed by thin aluminum bicyclists beginning their descent into the suburbs, their little libraries of locked hooks. A hill of uniformed questions will soon catch them in its searchlight file. Subject was not present so we proceeded without further hesitation. Pants unzipped, yank streets undone, dress flipped into the wind. His face was a wall where she wrote her name with teeth and stockings. This wooden cup we have dripped from their carriage of deleted stares. This warm red tusk we have pried from their garnished train schedule. All is recoded in our digital reference hook, should we need to tack them down.

In the story the man is writing with his left hand, one which is smaller and furrier than the one he uses to masturbate, a young couple enters the glass arcade of an abandoned subway station. She is behind the gleam of her transparent raincoat, while he is thrust in sleeves cut from a sequined dress. All through the glyphs and estuaries infiltrating his winter window, his large immaculate hand hovers in the air currents above where they are writhing on the cool marble floor. An impression of a rat peers at them from behind shorn posters advertising the highly lauded revival of a primitive circus, its promise of priapic

144

clowns prancing into the laws of her trapeze. Mouth clamps shut around ferrous stream. Nylon trigger pulls across first constraint button, its pink plastic wrist. He thinks "nipple" but writes "ripple" so as to avoid offending the classical figurines landing on the far side of the plumed lake, the ones with leather tassels flowing through lawns of engraved script.

The sun reflects off the far canyon wall, its rocks and candlelit shadows. Rows of grim, balding engravers imprint layers of suspended decay with crimson rust from another vanished civilization. Lines cut into the copper sky, their grooves interrupting contours of eyebrows and finger folded hands. Beneath the large winged shadow circling them, they invented disguises that led them away from their forfeits and bad descriptions. She wanted to be stained by the dust that collected in the lower precincts of his borrowed mouth, years of creosote and tallow gum. One of them tells the other, I will loosen them from my belt. Bends to it again. Ceremony swelling behind the eyes.

My girth inventory keeps spilling toward the power plant. I am a swivel tippet, a poinsettia hound. Someone is tapping the dream pipes behind the curtain separating them from planetary scans, slow thick waves creeping through the hairs. She likes to match the color of her lipstick and underwear, make him guess before burning his frown. The movie director has covered her face with titles, mouth stretched across the last consonants of signs fading into a book or drum, a cylinder whose external skin someone will sweep clean. Her dress aligns its skin to the vaults she keeps inside her special skit. Mucus stalls cost him a week's worth of mirrors.

A porno star named Gregor Samsa wakes up and discovers he has eight legs and two heads, one of which is laughing at the platinum prongs inserted between his polished mandibles. Gloved hands buff the burrs in his motion. Lag points in the falling air. The biker surrounded by feathers is instructed to incite picnics among the gathering shambles, spread blindness with a horn and rattle. A long list of possibilities clicks down. She chooses the first defiant flicker exposed to the reflections in her face.

She (or was it he dressed as she?) told them she was their residue growing into revenge, the saxophone plant rising through their floorboards and cotton guilt.

A rubber mote peeled off television's mechanized realism, its swimming pools and happy prowlers, its slave tablets and woolen shoves.

I unflag the hard smear I've spooned into the maw of my cellullar shadow, while she dials the controls of miasma patrol and asks them to alter the picture, its color heaps illuminating the bones behind the diagram. The concrete dance steps take us down to a new level in the garage expansion plan, moonlit storm behind a library tree, stuck in the cockpit of a plastic star, under the helmet of others. Visors etched with ancient curlicues.

She was all mouth and no eyes. He was three cancelled hands and a rented bed without adequate parking space. They were committed to the party that would remove history's claws from their parents' genitals. Absinthe stakes the heart to slower sonar blips in the blue of fright. She whispers: We will choose the slime in which to begin the next ledger. We will shovel off our stalks with yellow saddles. They were in the alley behind the Limbo Fields. He on his padded knees, needing. She wondering what other parts to raise on the screen.

They enter the pyramid, console controlled weather tipping its armature toward the modular woodshed near the central reserve nervous system. Guffaw signals stir inside the station, gusts of danger held at lurk distance. The buzzards tear at the gazelle, hyenas wait their turn. A lion and a lioness approach the wall the projectionist has mounted on the horizon, last rim before the beltway to paradise.

Relieve the intruder whose rubber knife never reaches the red button between her breasts, their sleek ripples adjusted to corrugated manipulators. Channel correction. He is forced to sprawl on his sleeves. A prickly tongue trails wet ruts in the sand clinging to the hairs growing on his forearms. Strips and then strips off.

Her blouse rises and falls with each rounded stave of music. The polished skull he keeps wrapped inside his best pants, their carved seams. In that space facing away, sometimes there. The here we enter and never speak about, the words sheltered in wood grain.

We wake up beneath the bench, beneath the lovers who do not notice us looking through the oval windows between them, counting the mineralized rings surrounding algae banks. Medicinal dusk spills across the pneumatic slag.

He pretended to be a butterfly and crouched in the dark. She told him he would have to wear her dress if he wanted what was inside. Blouse over partly opened face. Flattened moan dropped onto white rug. Three sided bed dressed in neck and wrists.

Choreographed preview complete with snippets of last week's written submissions. The wreck is flailing its tangerine possessions. Powdered stone tongue, slick delicate wisp. Blue sparks gathered in the grooves of his lower lip. This is the line you will have to cross, and this is the fine you will have to display. Ignore the clumps launched inside the clock, and find me, fine me, in the car's folding sled.

Her hands divided the room into available portions, the hexagons each of them would reveal. He knew it would be his last party when he climbed onto the stool and waited for the remaining paladins of contemporary ugliness to defile the cake with their exaggerated cheers.

The committee listed the provisions he could take with him when he entered the coliseum. Individuals have ceased to exist within the outer zones, replaced by webs of intersecting fleets. Their instructions: You must not trace the outlines of ghosts, nor follow the crumbs left by their radioactive footwear.

She opened her mouth, pushed the syringe into the deteriorating sky collecting on the ledges above the city. He stopped vacuuming the book with his tears, placed the nozzle between her sighs. I knew the corridor would eventually dissolve, that the dying would begin again. We are only matter in time, she whispered. I want to stay between the lines of our profiles, the gleam in the taxi window as we cross the bridge at midnight.

Fondle the imitation penknife beneath the streetlight. Read the sign that tells you what to rake off next. Extra days emerge from the hairless chambers at the bottom of a stencilled cup. Caressing one and then the other resting between their own hands. Gestures overturned in the dormant milk. A ceramic turnip floats near the floor or fleece. Heading north, just past the center of town, three jolly butchers raise their binoculars and focus on the turmoil spreading slowly through their aprons. One yaps, another yammers. Sawdust carriages clash above the salmon clouds.

Forbidden Entries III

The ones we once were wake up beneath the windowsill, beneath the lovers who do not notice them staring back, counting the bands roving their aisles of payment. Another romance shovel stuck in sound. I was one of a pair, he thought. And this thinking fled the suburbs of my extra bandage. Now I am a letter on a sign, a mirror filled with faces I never released.

Her pitcher held him captive and he could not get outside its porcelain shimmer. Face rounded into a mask. A ribbon of woodland music bleaching his fears.

The old robot enters the forest before anyone notices that it is missing. The beginning of the second fact. Her hands divide the room into the potions he would have to drain if he was to levitate his shadow above her welcome. All of this flows together. The audience shifts in their seats, unable to burn down the flights glancing at them from above their beds.

He made a fist which he glued to his sleeve. This will be a sign of my sign. The pools were dimpled. Individual bonuses ceased to exist for those who immigrated from the the outer provinces. Gems of dissected trails. Three days of hunger, it is how every bout begins. Dirty windows, noses pressed against dust and smear, tongues scraping glass. It was the first extra day of the month to appear in the calendar. They lopped off the surplus cradle. Dismembered herds, remembered words. The first time almost before landing. What did I think I was going to hear after the music faded? Lying beside her shadow dwelling in the hut of flight. Outside, two men in yellow bowling shirts fondle the nearest imitation glued beneath streetlight puddles.

Which one do I want to stay? Which wants to ventilate final twist. Remembers counting the pumps before grasping his handle. With and beside. Pants stained on wall above wigs. Read the sign that swells inside your glance. Under and near. Cry me a story, the river beneath these swarms of torrid goons. Do you think your sensitivity gauge is pointing its needle at me? When will it shift its treat toward the grove? Is this another rehearsal for giving? Secretion practice. Toward and behind. More lip motion is added. She tells me she expected a brittle rhumba, not flaccid hustle. Shows another fraction of what is glimpsed in the peel.

The lens of cigarette smoke spins toward us. Moisture pendant rips off gown. Neon trial and terror. Cocktail duress slips through her straps. The ones you used to dream about are still on parade. Drips out of plaid before sun reaches plant on windowsill. Names stuck to the ceiling of your youth. Pry them loose. What do you do with the bandages when there are no more slicks to stripe? The novice gushes into the piano. Full length body appeal. Did you drink this for its book? Do you remember the names you were given at the moment of entrance? My full round glass is the stage you will never mount. Hers, she said, meaning his and this. The words are pulled out of boats of steam. A row of gestures overturned in a river of milk. Floats near the floor squeezed from the screen. Dressing and washed. Modern fires bequeath their heights to a jar. Lies above the wink. On the lawn of a factory complex. In a park at midnight. Sandbox, backseat, under a stove. Blindfolded in a telephone booth. I agree with my face but nothing happens. What I found was all over my hands.

Forbidden Entries IV

The bridges suspended above the windows shook, welded pie wedges rippling beneath rumble of fleshy bulks and metallic franchises. His hand veered under the leaves of her fractional skirt, and began addressing her dampening thighs while fingering the rust infiltrating her nylon sheaths. She imagined him standing outside his shirt and pants, and decided to raise her left foot (trembling pendulum arch) and ask him for his telegenic mouth. If she was going to yield to the telemetry of his delicatessen surges, he needed to practice his oblations, their pink slip dance steps. It was the edge of summer's barn. They were trying to listen to the wires inside their heads when they heard the first insects clattering in the margins, waiting their turn.

Why paint doors and windows on walls of rooms we have all slept in, in dreams and elsewhere? Why frame its ocean? Or nail its sky to dented handle extending across longitudinal stains separating inside rings from outerwear? All is there, but you and I are here, at opposite ends of a room. A postcard would show this. The other side remaining blank. Or is it that I was for a long time afraid to write down what I had been told was a lie, something that doesn't happen anymore, not even between the pages of untread books.

First rule: You cannot use your tongue or tie your hands behind your back. Second rule: You cannot cast plaster flowers between breasts or thighs. Third rule: His and her dowels are out. There is no role to fill, no stall to bend around a river, its walls of slide. Nothing pulls you against her lips. They are a fiction, someone else's image bud, and you are the Keeper of

Lies. Fourth rule: Neither the act nor the motions though both are meshed together. Masks are out. Aphrodisiacs are another form of nostalgia.

Are you the subject or object or both? I was talking to the one who was writing, the one who would rather watch his hands or follow his eyes. He was consulting the tortoise shells piled before wallpaper rows of neatly stamped glands. One remedy is to accept the dried penis of a white horse soaked in honey and wine. Grind dragon fossils opalized in many colors to ride the ceiling of ghosts. Drink rainwater on the first day of spring before entering black and gold chamber. These are the ravings of a scribe wandering in the hive, he said. A scrofulous paw smattered these dictums down. I am a historian of an exquisitely gowned window or wind, the slippery panes between the shimmer of their exhalations. Rose madder sunlight of office windows across the river, what we saw later. They were there as movie candles, molten lug nuts in the bubbling gyre.

I thought about this as the room shifted, tremors and aftershocks, the bridge swaying into the field of glow. It was not I who was thinking these perimeters, but the ones who were thinking me into this space, delirious buzz sloping down to a pit of rumpled squalls.

I got up and turned back the clocks of the moon. You were languishing in the chair of your moistened lap, adjacent to the brass claws of a cluttered platform. It was not a pose stiffened into paint. It was not a prism twisting at the end of a corporeal bell. I saw this then, hear it buzzing now in the precincts of my porcelain toupee, the canopy on which I incised these anthracite hieroglyphs. Encircled rubber staff, flensed whale. I poll the dice cakes, their rows of grinning monkeys measuring the twilight of another discarded tribute.

Triumph of lightning. We were dancing in the hallway

between bad dreams, empty subway cars hovering above the windows overlooking empty sheets, their embroidered instructions. Drone stings hammered down the sky, its charcoal shutters closed to the scenic flow. We were beneath that and each other. Time and circumstance are enclosures, the original pyramid of lifts and thrusts eludes the shore of today's drugstore light, its fallow mound of aspirin substitutes. You remember yourself beginning at the tip of the edge of the flesh quivering back. A stem glides by. More so now that imported sand is skittering across the floor. Something else besides bottled air is leaving the marquee. One day I will be too old to remember my name, flesh lumped on a stainless wooden tray for others to kiss. Another decaying wing added to the pile.

I could list the articles of clothing as I first saw them, the verbs they held. Past participles in the present perfect. Cascade tongue delving between their layers. Snake skin lava invading the gridded calm. A stoop of drops tapping through the calcified din. Libertine polydactyl extract dissolving the borders. To be in the middle of all this and feel your way toward the front, hands and feet, word by word.

She wandered into my mouth, peeled back the pages, and showed me her spine of blistering glue. Red emissions fluttered to the roof of her glance. I reached inside, pried the wet butterfly loose. A pond in the middle of the wall began spilling against the slides, their accumulations of vagrant detail filling the margins with gelatinous color. We didn't need a camera to take them, she said. We don't need to remember when we can go on. She was circling her crouch of ribboned groans, telling me to ram her through the pages stained with yesterday's blood. A soft splash briefly shielded us from the author's memories. I didn't ask. You didn't tell. We switched tides. Will we talk about that? Will we mention the room in which we placed ourselves at each other's disposal? Will I foreshorten its walls? Open its sides to the glare?

The moon is a caliper folded in foam. I am lying beside the cellar window, a blue cathode ray tube interrogating the chalcedony flakes I hold in my hands. She scratches the hollow door with her hair. She is wearing a bathrobe she has taken from her husband's closet. Cinched tight and high against the push. She wants me to stir something up, something larger than anger. This is the flush. And this is the scene of the crime, she whispers. I want you to scour it for evidence.

I saw her staked beneath a street lamp. We were alone. Everyone else was watching the movie. We burrowed deeper into the stale velvet plush. My fingers reached the first hedge of tropical erosion. I am refueling my brains, she hummed. I am the recipient of all your incisions. Would you like to try this on for size? She was spilling milk with her eyes. Her coat was blue and laced with pockets, leather flaps for my hands to grip its windows, steer inside. I pulled myself up. I stood and waited for her to burn sounds. Pleasant odors entered our secretions, their cakes and jellies. I told I was on my way to dust when she ordered me to drink the sweet lotion of rhyme, and then break its vowels against her finely hammered lips.

The gauze of this scratch, the haze of this asphalt bench. From corroboree to couvade, from hammocks to handcuffs. Unfastened plums grew moth lungs on the outskirts of the mattress. I swallowed a deer. I slept in a tree. I counted the arrows piercing skin. Python bile clung to the wax of my human pliers. I began to dance, though some still call it an affliction.

You turn from the window and make a sign. The map leads us back to the treadmill gropes. Why enter a fairy tale proscenium when there is further madness to pursue, an outpost, station or mound of shifting crusts beyond any we might remember? I am a rogue ant who distrust treatises. I am a pair of carbon gongs swimming in muddles of milk and benzedrine, a row of little slosh cakes mopping up the gush of now. Thirst shifts to my tongue again, follows itself down. I taste the tremble.

Forbidden Entries V

The Second Sign is usually made of stolen cinnabar:

Large red handprints on inner walls of wet thighs. Granular sift through porous identity stamp. Tell-tale smudges, cascading hair. Eyes twisting on stems, unexplained neural discharges. Sudden outbreaks of fiery glints. Meanwhile, two rocks shunt crystallized glimmers of dense artificial light through five remaining ceremonial circuits or the "Ace of Clouds."

Unbeknownst to the inner ring of barefoot dancers, their interior circumstances have been re-routed through the veins of an archway materializing in the lower pouches of the physical plane.

Some persist in using the old term, "mandible bunching."

What happened. A few reels of ooze followed by unfamiliar motion mishap. Muscle blots and poor visibility began impeding spotted rainbow effect.

First Report: gaseous splendor infiltrates perforated anatomy, columns of wet sand spill from handcrafted leather beaks.

Second Report: An old movie theater on edge of deserted city. Ripped velvet riders. The span of light on which writhing unravels is accompanied by whirr of insect wings, incessant drumming.

Third report: The programmed "I" sent into decorative cave is unable to interrupt anonymous broadcasts. Inner courtyard is sealed off. Tiles removed and transported to temple sanctuary for further inspection.

Memory machines take notes, measure dimensions, calculate probability factor.

Large vertical sections of pseudo-sexual narratives are still being transmitted to those who signed up for maiden voyage.

Stuck in the crave of their illicit folding—empty envelopes, slick meat wrappers, old gum bars, substitute locks. Jars of unknown substance left by door.

Amnesiac mutes use bones and feathers to describe combustion levels of external dreams.

> *Purification through*
> *Reptilian coiling*
> *Butterfly gateway opens*

The first wave of rehabilitated sleepers begins blinking, drugged orbs spinning, like iridescent beetles beneath eyelids' crimson turtle shells. Tongues dry, swollen. Hands unable to close.

> *Somewhere during the fourth night of the outlaw tale,*
> *in a hidden alley or unmapped cul-de-sac,*
> *the last remnants of an ancient cult*
> *begin raising fever levels*
> *above horizon of blue zigzag lightning lines*
> *painted on voyagers' chests*
> *until redesigned implants take effect,*
> *and second level nocturnal trellises*
> *can halt progress of artificial stars,*
> *split story into seedlings.*

Deeper examinations are taking place in lobby, beneath and between gathered husks, outlines left by the dancers.

We have been ordered to go in and find them, capture the shifts and collisions, the dances we intuited from the fragments drifting across the desert, the curtain of mirages stained with perfume and sweat.

The inhabited shadows wait.
We don't tell our superiors what we suspect, because they would return us to the department store, market us as the latest examples of *Imitation Contraband*.

Forbidden Entries VI

Wire adjustments and battery update. The bathers ignore the clouds of radio-activated fish gathering by their feet. There are two of them standing waist high in a trench of speckled water, though each now believes that once the moon begins to slip behind the long glove of smoke nailed to the western sky, its windowsills of glittering dirt, the ones nestled inside inlaid cups and calfskin harnesses will be able to emerge, unvarnished writhers in the scalloped spill of blue shadows.

This, we tell ourselves, is the place where we must start, our hands plunging into the ink splashing over each event.

Their eyes are cameras tracking flesh's acoustic indicators, mounds of untapped imaging transmitters wired along the dorsal and ventricle muscles shifting and surging blood pounding memory's door.

One of us is opening his or her eyes, one's identity still unknown. Perhaps sight will tell us how to approach the body each of us inhabits. How are we to know if this is not this? What is this this? a voice at the back of the room or skull insinuates. The question relieves us of the need to answer.

They had been elected to leave the pit and point their way past the inlet of burning pleasure boats. They were told that once they left, they could remove their masks and air filtration tanks.

Inventory of necessary items: Four sets of double rowed metal claws, two reusable elastic evening gowns, extra bag of emerald sequins, diamond choker, black rubber-like pants, green alligator shoes, three flashlights, and a well-thumbed manual illustrating the positions they could utilize their hidden bodies to assemble beneath a powdery sky, enervated stars imbedded in snake paths of winter's soot.

Repeated intersections of projected bodies would form the oracle's messages on chalk cliffs demarcating horizon. They would have to learn the dimensions they could unfold.

The one who is blindfolded moans in direct proportion to the pyramids being erected between his (or her) thighs. About this distinction the narrator was never clear.

All this happened before our last narrator died, an extinguished mineral light, and no one has been able to assume the notational interstices of flesh-like appearances that have been periodically transmitted to this camouflaged well.

Who could be sent out to discover where the verbs had settled? Who would know how to translate the diagram of levers and weights?

The great parcel shift left us with pronouns turning to ash in the hands of those foolish to use them as pointers. *Had the narrator said this would happen?*

In some instances, we could say *who* but we couldn't say *what.* In other instances, equally difficult to sort out, we could say *what* but not *who.*

A story with names falls into both categories, and cannot be repeated without an elaborate punishment or *peregrine liturgy* sealed in wax, perfumed by the executioner.

Out there, slipping between quilted layers of smoke
Out there, on a metal card table beneath lightbulb sun
Out there, within scope-sight of barbed wire
its shiny thorns and rusted roses
a blazing shadow rises

Forbidden Entries VII

I have not encountered this variant of fur before. A swill of fetid rumors rising from my new titanium claws, their velvet handles. What effect will this have upon the terminals clustered along my outer ridges? Is there a device to ward off microbe storms bubbling within the pockets of accumulation gathered beneath horizon? I drop down from my assigned position and transmit three alternatives: *Buddha's Delay, Promiscuous Kidnap,* or *Goblin Manger.* No reply.

The three remaining crew members are puddled in front of a disconnected celestial clock, their signal flags mounted on a tree of plastic medallions which entitle the bearer to a Free Extra Large Meal Bag, the kind you are rewarded after completing enough journeys to the outer beltway of dense mining colonies. Five moons on burning bush of upper atmosphere, each of them leaking sickness particles into the air's paltry remains. Broken funnel between the ones on the ground and the ones listening for first signs of the queen's persimmon obligatto. A figure of unknown species shimmers in the window of pollution between them, breasts suspended in grasp of an open stare.

Tiger-striped heat ripples through last rows of cannisters stacked behind billboard of rusted empire. Searchlight sequence yields a few shadows accompanying pouches of holy dust. The one without clothes, soft skin covered in yellow down, is shimmying to the neo-classical refrains implanted in decaying cortex. A hand reaches down between and pries apart. The length of each moan is measured and added to the music through a cellullar loop. Caterwauls in the park.

162

Tingling down TV attennae perks the watchers, their double contact lined eyes glistening with tiny nodules.

Nerve stubs register the possibility of it and its twin being leisure replacement vehicles. Is this a way to latch them in suits, rubber armed ditchers ready to toss the flags over their pried faces? Fleshy appendage slithers across dented bed, sweat dials grinning behind numbered spots. Glass decanters hidden in valleys of old hair conditioner masks. I, a cool mimetic voice whispers, need to grunt down a little slab before she turns her wheel. A section at a time might begin to appease the waves of hunger surging through my sanitized rings, turnstile video outfits running loose in monasteries and malls. Voice bubbles burst above his leather head.

She squeezes her lotion. Licks tube with long blue tongs. Lures insects toward mirror, where they might see themselves losing flight. Edible sequence edited from final production. Children warned to look away, out windows, down alleys, where moths beat the dust into mounted foreheads of the wall. News of its existence begins seeping through walls and floors. Each version embosses a different plane of contact. Furry initiates howl for proof.

His hands begin swelling in the stork stretch between suburban street and two star garage. It has locked him in its mouth, new flows of bristled teeth glistening around his empty projectile. Gasps spill onto her hair, blue macaroni strands fitted with halos of arctic fur. Bicycle pump in corner of screen, empty garbage cans, two bags filled with plastic leaves, all that's left from party that never burst through panel door. Slide periscope over, raise charms in air. Unclasp and release. Another quadrant secured for further probing.

The avalanche is automatically slowed down and guided to the loading dock. Inspection of trajectory, weight, and shape begins. Turnstile tragedy broadcast through amber voice box. Rented voters spin the statistical rise in decaying romantic splatter against recent government decree. The mind is a robot which fails to listen to its commands.

VII

In Between and Around

And all the while we were kissing,
the two of us, and the many we are,
were standing, kneeling, or spinning
upside down in the long wet arms of prayer,
waiting to be kissed.
Pimply slumps of pockmarked muscles.
Closet behind schoolyard
back alley train station
midnight morning
lifts through blue light
locked inside eyes and breath
held in wet palms.
Hands and mouth gripping.
All paws and fur.
Tepid tongue, slippery teeth.
First joyful snake stabs.
All the while we were kissing
on a dusty summer afternoon,
someone was standing outside us,
watching our shadows perpetrate a body
on soft asphalt beneath cloudless sky.
Walking, as if there is somewhere to go.
Petulant scowl, lips that flower,
scorched red petals swelling
neither to be caressed nor plucked.
Waiting all the while for the ones
inside us who are kissing
to see the ones who are there,
behind and before,
the ones without boundaries

and the places opening within.
The ones pushing and pushing
against words and air
and the beams of light lodged between them,
as if all doors would open
and the form presently inhabited
would be released into a dimension
from which there is no return,
particles and wavelengths
flowing through each other.
One of them thinking, always afraid
to fill a thought with words, breathe
outside the boundaries of the third person,
though eyes in hazy half-light
watch the lips parting with each breath,
and the body beside the one
who is sleeping sweats.
The sweat rolling down the face
mingles with tears, and the tears
moisten the lips. The lips of the one
who wished and waited and finally spoke
or the lips of the one who wouldn't and didn't.
Rows of mouths, closed or twisted,
open or shut in dunes and curtains
flowering under the monument's hammer.
Of these tears and the tears beside them,
the ones about which you cannot speak
and are afraid to see, of these and others
the *Book of Trembling* is written.
Flailing hands, unraveling hair.
Hands sliding around each other
like scarves unable to form a knot
or a knot unable to be loosened.
A pond flecked with summer's last daubs.
And the body one sees beneath
and within the fabric rustling

and shifting with every breath
drawn across the taut sweep of skin,
eyes fixated, air held in lungs,
smoldering there, the sounds
swelling louder and louder
than the thoughts releasing them.
All the while the voices are rising
towards one's mouth, borrowed, broken,
or temporarily possessed, two tremulous
ropes are kissing behind and beyond
the ones who are crawling, shifting
away from and towards,
near and under and beside
this around nearing and nearer.
Sometimes a pleasant shrieking,
gurgles and wriggling gasps.
A sigh like that of one in pain.
And all the while the ones
we imagine ourselves to be
go on kissing and kissing,
hands prying apart,
fingers squeezing
twisting hard buttons,
plucking at metal and cloth,
and the rippling overlap of two
consecutive, stretching, pushing forms
located on the physical plane
between liquid and solid disintegrates
the dorsal trajectories,
as they go on,
as if that is all they can do,
the only place of sustenance
being where their mouths mesh,
all they want being the mouth
opening and closing around, over, and between.
And the kissing goes on

even when the body grows lax,
soft and malleable as a spoon of lead or wax,
something to thud against the wind.
And the wind moves aside,
as the kissing continues,
and the mouths move aside,
as the bodies become plants
on the ocean floor, spinning within
the motions of air's sweet tremors.
And the kissing begins to take hold,
while inside the ones who are kissing,
the ones whose mouths have merged
into a single speaker of divided thoughts,
are other mouths, hands, and feet.
And their voices begin rising, expanding,
and there is no end to the clamoring, whispers,
whistles, mumbles, and screams,
while the ones who are kissing go on
because there is nothing and nowhere else,
no other hospital but here
where lips are meeting.
Shoulders, arms, fingers, eyelids,
and elbows join with feet, ribcage, and legs,
Mouths open, words or sounds
resembling words emerge
and melt among sounds of cars honking,
curses of the hurt and shunned,
tremors of astronauts dreaming,
sunlight drifting across shutters.
And the sounds of the kissing
reach the ones lined up inside
waiting to be kissed.
Some feel a mouth or mouths,
and others don't,
while the shadows
in the hallway their bodies form

keep kissing, lips
pressing and pushing against lips,
teeth and tongue.
And sometimes a voice tells them
they are the silhouettes of the ones
waiting, wanting, refusing, afraid
of the kissing that goes on and on,
and the kissing that brings
something more, something else,
the kissing that is just
a sign of what will happen,
a taste or touch.
Murmurs leading to tremors
and more kissing
piled on top of the kisses.
Having watched, having seen.
After before and during a kiss
that never begins.
And this voice whispers
about the taste or touch
that some mouths never know
and about which they cannot speak,
having never tasted or been tasted.
The one tied to the chair obtained by the family.
The one strapped in the chair provided by the state.
And all that they have to say about kissing
that has never been heard by those who have kissed,
and the ones trying not to hear what all the ones
inside them are saying,
thought bending to mouth
whose mouth is being met is now.
All the while.

VIII

DREAM HOSPITAL

Dream Hospital I

One eye opens. Above it a cloud. Rounded edges where it clings to the wall like wet lips pressed against a window, its ridged imprint. A single occupancy bed, crumpled swirl of gray waves and a string of quivers and eruptions. Meanwhile, the other eye circles beneath the rubbery shell of flesh clamped over its pierced dome.

A log cabin with three bunk beds in one room and a double bed in the other. The parents sleep in the big bed, the one as wide as the Texas Panhandle, soft as cotton candy. The kind of bed you can burrow into. Gopher mush.

Usually, the four children sleep neatly in two bunks, and the third bunk is reserved for friends and sleep-overs. The parents issue each child two sets of blankets. The pale pink and blue ones are divided according to gender, and the fear of being teased, while the khaki army blankets fit all sizes and shapes, knees, nubs, and breasts. The embarrassing dangle.

The two boys are ages nine and twelve, and the two girls are ten and sixteen. Twenty years later, you will be the oldest boy, one eye open, watching his sister climb out of top bunk and into the lower one where her boyfriend is lying on his back. She will pull up her pink flannel nightgown and straddle him. Only you will be sitting by a window in Greenwich Village, looking into an apartment across the street. You have a front row seat. The room is painted persimmon. There's a bureau, a bed, and a wicker chair. The closet door is open. A full length mirror has been affixed to it.

You are waiting for the man in the other room to finish talking on the phone. On the screen, and across the street, a young woman begins dressing. She changes her mind and goes through the bureau, looking for the right piece of lingerie. Bends, turns, stretches, and examines.

The older brother was staring down from the top bunk on the other side of the room, one eye, like a frog, motionless. The two of you were smiling. It was nearly dawn and birds were chirping in the tall pines surrounding the cabin at the edge of a lake. You acted as if you didn't know he was watching.

She is standing with her back to you, looking in the mirror. You are leaning on your elbows, binoculars pressed against your face, a harness. Summer evening. Both windows are open. In the mirror she sees herself and perhaps an oval shadow in the window across the street. A black mirror or hole in the atmosphere.

After getting dressed, and satisfied with her packaging, she leaves the apartment and goes downstairs. She stands on the stoop, looks up at the window where you are sitting and smiles briefly. A tiny, almost imperceptible shrug flares in her shoulders and echoes its way down muscles and ribcage. She taps her right foot—she's wearing bright blue high heels—then stops, and goes down to the street and hails a cab. Gleam of ankle bracelet. The man has gotten off the phone and is standing in the doorway. He asks you if you've enjoyed the scenery. You answer in the affirmative.

After a few minutes, she ascended to her bunk, leaned over the side and winked. Her long brown hair fell like a curtain you wished would touch the floor. You heard her brother roll over, face the wall. Before the sun climbed above the horizon, someone would get up and go to the bathroom, and someone else would masturbate.

176

This movie was never shown again, and its director is not listed in any of the guides or encyclopedias. You and the others in this film have gone on to play numerous other roles, and, as yet, none of them are memorable in quite the same way.

Dream Hospital II

Mouth maybe

A voice taking shape
in the interior precincts

Webbed window of broadcasts
Floating and turning

Inside or outside not known

A tape recorder is on, and the session has started

I'm the sole resident of a room which is smaller than a box

The source of the voice hasn't been detected

My head I keep hidden behind the far wall
its feathers of blue smoke

Perhaps there's more than one and they are talking to each
     other

I call this room a book or a story
calibrated rectangles closing around a voice

archways of roses drifting beneath
the streetlamp's cloudy yellow eye

At the other end of the maze is a castle
lined with cordovan shoes and patent leather heels

This is the second time I have told a lie

The latest snakeskin trophy is mounted on a nail
just inside the iron door

This is the first time I have told the truth.

I predict hands will swing down from a smelly cloud

Memorize geological formation of the body
its topography of insults

I live in a box made of rooms
none of which tells the complete story

How many years did I (or someone like me)
spend under the table, looking up

I (or any other corner to which I was sent)
was a scribe of orchestrated gestures

a sentinel stowed in a cage
My companion: A trim satyr

in pressed gaberdine
his left hoof enthralled by the music

tinkling in his cartridge head
that broad balcony where Juliet's ghost never roamed

I dreamed that she was slim and pale, dusky and tall
the color of a peach before the sun grabs its throat

Calf muscles honed on the lathe of a bicycle
Dance of roots reaching beneath the earth

Left hoof swirling like a compass
Trim toenails, red moons rising

I slept in a forest of geometric legs
wooden chairs cut in the shape of penitence

Four unyielding trunks of prayer
rising toward the platform where a worshipper sat

urging himself to become a robe of purple grass
Now I'm repeating the unspoken

doctrine of the body's transformative orbit
It is one of the voices my pronouns broadcast

The goal: Become a blanket where worms roll
in a chorus of grooves cut by a dry wind

and sparrows of rain sway beyond
the horizon's whiskey colored glass

The goal: Become something you are not
a shadow or the bicycle of a shadow

pedaling down an empty street
green and gray envelopes of sunlight

in the glossy postcard distance
I am a window overlooking myself

It is why I have eyes in the back of my head
why I can see the forest fire

I am trying to leave behind
Hands swimming toward the surface

feet pressing against
the linoleum earth

the body a rope
twisting between

these gravitational sockets

Dream Hospital III

I consult a pleasure map
floating on the other side

of the moon or its mop
their handles pointed

at the puzzle
you call your heart

I live in a room facing
all the clouds or clods

I have ever counted
Bright chips of cheap flutter

in the outer rings of
interrogatory drift

Dogs once stalked
this latch of rusted earth

but now all I fear are voices
stirring behind the blanket of stars

I am a tube lump
stowed in the terraced dark

I am the front of a fiend
and the crumpled bag

following him to the three corners
when all else falls away

I am one of the stalls in which you hide
the details of your mechanized brain

Dream Hospital IV

Why listen to the little blabber mouse proudly striding around the rim of your visor? Haven't you pulled its bright grating down over your eyes yet? Haven't you placed yourself inside the pool of warm shadows collecting along the base of the wall? When will you start folding yourself into yourself? The questions form a stump in your battered coat. Cold sparks splash against the floor.

Either I'm dreaming that I'm in a hospital or I'm in a hospital and I'm dreaming. The main doors open in both directions but the portholes do not. One must signal before entering or exiting the dumping grounds. Grainy mop handles rest precariously against grimy pails. Train tracks of dirty water, hot bubbles fulminating within. Rows of mismatched slippers. Remedial odors lingering above the inverted bottles.

The person in the next bed is writing furiously. Chalk shovel scraping hard surface followed by moments of manic erasing. Clouds dissipated by machine gun bursts of wind spraying the auditorium where we have been deposited.

You can hear yourself chewing the certified slush the nurses bring you in covered dishes. A spoon that swivels in your mouth. You are sure the others can hear you, a marching band of crooked teeth shaping the little balls of clay nearly everyone has obediently inserted in their clammy maws. A voice assures you: The noise in your head has always been there. Do not silence this candle. You look for the body that possesses this speaking contraption. The noise and the voice producing it shifts to another station, which is interrupted by flakes of falling plaster. Heaven, the nurse announces, is releasing its letters. Each of you will soon be receiving the news you've been waiting for.

Dream Hospital V
(for Eric Peterson)

She walks by the window of the cafe where you and a friend have been sitting for a few hours, discussing in some oblique way your definitions of love. It is past midnight and the both of you have been looking intently out the window, seeing what snippets of drama you might get to witness. You wave to her to come in and she blows you a kiss but then stops, turns around, and enters the otherwise empty cafe. She walks over to your table, stands behind your chair, as if you needed to be pushed in closer.

Introductions, synopses of present occupations, all quickly and efficiently accomplished. She is co-writing a film script about a famous body builder and doesn't have a job. Her partner once edited an interview you conducted with a musician you first heard when you were seventeen. You don't mention this because you don't want to interrupt her. She moved out of a place where writing is done for no money and landed elsewhere. Writing and money should shake hands every chance they get, she says. Sitting there, the two of you nod and smile. You agree and disagree, the world is not ideal.

In a week your friend is returning to Minnesota, near the Canadian border, to chop wood for his parents, before returning to Albuquerque to finish school. You met him a few months ago, in Albuquerque. Cold windy day on the plains. Long gray clouds lit from behind by a yellow sun. You and she were in the same class. Down the street from *Bow Wow Music* in a diner where his brother spotted you ordering breakfast. A motel, no outgoing calls. He wrote you a letter and you

186

answered it. Is there such a thing as "Albuquerque Sound?" Boston 1967: *Ultimate Spinach*. What was the name of the drummer who lost his left hand in an accident and held the stick with a shiny hook? Played in *The Barbarians*. You remember your friend and his older brother who recently published a book on Robert Johnson. Not all of this is said but there is a lot of laughter to fill in those intervals of silence where the three of you pull back into yourselves, remembering.

Things left out. The night she and her friend and you got in the same bed, in a small room on the sixth floor of an apartment overlooking a parochial school. She went to sleep or so she said. Her friend and you did not, eyes open, staring across the inches separating you. Hands brushing against, over. Flutter of tentative caresses. She woke up, must have sensed why the two of you were facing each other, were so physically close, and said she was going home. She needed to be in her own bed, needed some sleep. Her friend stayed, said she was too tired to move.

A few months earlier (or was it later) you went to her apartment, and the two of you ended up in her bed. Down comforter. Empty bottles of wine strewn across the floor. This time, the only time it turned out, she was the one who was leaving, and it wasn't morning yet. You and her friend, who you've been told is now married to a man in Virginia, talked about making love and then made love without talking. She wanted to do it she said but that would be the end of it. No calls, no further contact. Her name is unusual but not unique. One morning, while reading a book of poems by a young woman who you know is dying of an incurable disease, you stopped, jerked back in your chair because you put these two women together. The same name. The woman who spent one night in your apartment, and the woman whose book you now own.

Dream Hospital VI

Between prefabricated motels, their pastel stained fresco walls, in the alley running down to the ocean, a pack of spotted dogs is gnawing on a simulated version of my body. Before I can figure out the coordinates where I've suddenly coalesced, and become an ambulatory cone of fleshy sludge, I receive a telepathic communication from my rubber encased control panel. I am instructed not to panic. For reasons I don't yet understand, I decide this judgement is the most prudent one and begin inspecting the premises. The walls are covered with squares of plucked fur, trophies left by previous guests. The mirrors extending through the portholes to whatever begin their predetermined rotation. At last, I can see the ocean has started pulling away from the shore.

I'm trying to decipher a row of dials when the phone rings and a voice announces, it's 8:30. I'm not sure whether it's morning or night since clumps of atmosphere are peeling off the window, leaving a sky full of either holes or jagged disks. Nothing is glowing, though all the planes have been penetrated by particles of illuminated matter. Although the light is blue, I cannot fit it into any of the sequences I still remember.

Another voice fume leaks out of the miniature television, suggesting that if I go into another room of the dream, I'll find the door separating me from the alley and my body. I decide it's easier to stay inside, away from the dogs whose snarls are starting to sound familiar, like nicknames you'd rather forget. The sky has become a leopard of rippling black asteroids. Clouds are being yanked back into their holes. Someone is stammering in his grave.

188

I find it is easier to walk backwards, registering all the nooks and crannies ("crooks and nannies") of proficient industry something resembling my body just filled. What borrowed thing have I replaced it with? What necessity? Perhaps everything will return to its proper niche if I swim in reverse. Perhaps my body will be returned to me, intact. Why mount your shadow on a hook? I ask, knowing I have finally spoken out of turn.

I slink towards the kitchen. Time has become a revolving door without a house or a street to buttress my suspicions about the past or future. Walled cities recede into the surrounding mirage. A memory card is inserted into my lower left quadrant. The reprogramming has commenced.

A large bean on a silver plate and no one to share it with. Soon I'll be sitting beside myself, talking and eating. Soon I'll be arriving at the place where I first set out, a cold dark room, before all this began.

IX

Double Agent I

Who can say we did not take turns
encouraging another pronoun to grow between us,

pretended not to see its storm
sprout into a he or a she

an it or a that, bulbous lump or lamp
punching a tunnel through a scream's decorated arcades,

but now it becomes this: *As each pronoun propels itself*
     forward,
into the zone once called "the future,"

on the steam of its own words.
And which of those pronouns said:

A city of attentive hands will bubble up on the horizon,
a large red moon mounted on one of its towers.

Now that all the tears have been gathered and counted.
I will be the one who cuts them down from the sky,

forges them into a silver necklace.
I will be the one who will turn your tears into a dowry,

which I shall keep, as I keep you,
warm and soft in my gravel hands.

These scratches will make you glisten.
These cuts will help you shine.

The one who says: O string of blue emblems
glowing in memory of your own iridescent demise.

The one who says: My hands are kept in iron boxes.
The key is taped to the bottom of my tongue.

The one who says: Soon the pronouns will shift
their mirrors, swing open their arms.

Interior and exterior dimensions
will infiltrate the formulas

governing the remnants of old stories,
their colonies of migrating poison.

Yes, there will be many to choose from,
and all of them will fit.

The one who says: The things I did to turn you into a ghost
kept you in its shiny locket,

the one I wore when I left the house,
left you mired in dusk's gathering pond.

The one who promises: One day we might find ourselves
and each other there, in a room small enough for two.

The one who says: You know only half the story,
the other half I wrote when you weren't looking.

Even if you could lick all the words,
the ink will never fade.

The one who says: The insects swimming through the wind
      caught in your hair
are all that's left of yesterday's stars.

194

This is the bridge you must cross,
the window you must open.

The one who says: I vacated you and then I came back.
Why didn't you let me go.

And the shadow who answers:
You were neither my house nor horse.

The one who says: You will forget each word
as soon as you reach the next one.

You will spit the same word into a hat over and over again.
You will be banished from the Cave of Witnesses.

The one who says: Why cling to the stem
until it rots in your mouth.

Double Agent II

In each of us resides a popular medalist
and an author of a grim little volume

No mathematician has been able to subtract
this volcanic assertion

from the Island of Obsolete Dread
that uncoiled theme park

where our parents kissed
the syphillitic face of their first jolt

You must try not to mishandle my apparatus
when I want all of us to inhabit a soft ballet

They used to bring him back in a wheelbarrow
Perhaps now a silk cable will do the trick

One was loaded with imported booze
the other was dumped in antique ooze

I don't think the sky can become more persuasive
Why do you need to fabricate other alternatives

What do you mean you forgot how to embrace
Here, put these bulbs in your mouth

and climb yonder silo tree
because the only scheme I have up my sleeve is you

How many times have I sagged
against our last drum of electricity

Just because we are fragments of fragments
doesn't mean we have to fall apart

track the plaster trickling from
the corners of our eye patches

Traces of their oodles are still visible
in the blisters of the hotel carpet

Do you want to make this into a pilgrimmage
Might we not also want to try

and assemble a magnet
which will hypnotize us

into believing what we say

Double Agent III

You said
I want to walk into mirrors with you

But the only mirror you pointed to
was a blue shield

engraved with all the lies
growing inside the you

you presented to the world
its icy blur

You said
We are prisoners of something larger

than our respective stories
It is a storm whose clouds are covering my mouth

with the fingers
I once pried off a book

its ventilated pages
its slender installments of condensed exhalations

You said
I ate the chapter I wrote

and spit out the one I read
the one you thought we were writing

beneath the mirror
we pretended to glue to the sky

Printed October 1996 in Santa Barbara
& Ann Arbor for the Black Sparrow Press by
Mackintosh Typography & Edwards Brothers Inc.
Text set in Galliard by Words Worth.
Design by Barbara Martin.
This edition is published in paper wrappers;
there are 200 hardcover trade copies;
100 hardcover copies have been numbered & signed
by the author; & 20 copies lettered A to T
have been handbound in boards
by Earle Gray & are signed by the author.

PHOTO: Eve Aschheim

JOHN YAU is a poet, fiction writer, and critic who has written extensively on contemporary art. He has taught at various colleges and universities, most recently at Brown University, the University of California, Berkeley, and Hofstra University. He has received fellowships and grants from the National Endowment for the Arts, the Ingram-Merrill Foundation, and the New York Foundation for the Arts, and been awarded a General Electric Foundation Award, a Lavan Award (Academy of American Poets), the Brendan Gill Award, and the Jerome Shestack Prize (*American Poetry Review*). As Ahmanson Curatorial Fellow (1993–96), he organized a Retrospective of paintings and drawings by Ed Moses, which opened at the Museum of Contemporary Art, Los Angeles in the Spring of 1996. He lives in Manhattan. Current projects include a memoir, fiction, and research for a book on the silent film actress Anna May Wong.